REAL
SALVATION

Register This New Book

Benefits of Registering*

- ✓ FREE **replacements** of lost or damaged books
- ✓ FREE **audiobook** – *Pilgrim's Progress,* audiobook edition
- ✓ FREE information about new titles and other **freebies**

www.anekopress.com/new-book-registration

*See our website for requirements and limitations.

REAL
SALVATION

AND WHOLE-HEARTED
SERVICE FOR THE LORD

Reuben A. Torrey

We enjoy hearing from our readers. Please contact us at www.anekopress.com/questions-comments with any questions, comments, or suggestions.

Aneko Press

www.anekopress.com

Aneko Press, Life Sentence Publishing, and our logos are trademarks of

Life Sentence Publishing, Inc.
203 E. Birch Street
P.O. Box 652
Abbotsford, WI 54405

RELIGION / Christian Theology / Soteriology

Paperback ISBN: 978-1-62245-651-2

eBook ISBN: 978-1-62245-652-9

10   9   8   7   6   5   4   3

Available where books are sold

Contents

Chapter 1

Where Art Thou?

Where art thou? (Genesis 3:9)

My subject here is the first question that God ever asked of man. You will find that question in Genesis 3:9: *Where art thou?* God asked the question of Adam. Adam had sinned, and on the evening of that awful day of the first sin, the voice of God in its majesty was heard rolling down the avenues of the garden of Eden. Adam had often heard God's voice before, and the voice of God had been the sweetest music to Adam until this day. Adam knew no greater joy than the glad communion with his Creator and his heavenly Father. But now all was different, and as the voice of God was heard rolling through the garden, Adam was filled with fear and tried to hide himself.

That is the history of every son of Adam from that day until now. When sin enters our hearts and our lives, we seek to hide from God. Every sinner is trying to hide from the presence and the all-seeing eye of God. That accounts for a very large share of the skepticism, infidelity, agnosticism, and atheism of our day. Sinful man is trying to hide from a holy God.

Men will give you many reasons why they are skeptics, and many reasons why they are infidels, agnostics, and atheists, but in the great majority of cases the real reason is that by the denial of the existence of God, men hope to hide themselves from the discomfort of God's acknowledged presence. That accounts also for much of the neglect of the Bible. People will tell you that they do not read their Bibles because they have so much else to read and are not interested in the Bible. They will say it is a dull, stupid book to them; but the real cause of man's neglect of Bible study is that the Bible brings God near to us as no other book does, and men are uneasy in the conscious presence of God, so they neglect the book that brings God near.

This also accounts for much of the absenteeism from the house of God and its services. People will give you many reasons why they do not attend church. They will tell you they cannot dress well enough to attend church, that they are too busy and too tired to attend church, that the services are dull and uninteresting. But **No man ever succeeded in hiding from God.** in the great majority of cases, the reason men and women, old and young, habitually avoid church services is that the church brings God near and makes men uncomfortable in sin. Their desire to hide from God, more or less distinct, leads them to stay away from church.

But Adam did not succeed in hiding from God. Neither will you succeed. No man ever succeeded in hiding from God. God said to Adam, *Where art thou?* and Adam had to come out from his hiding place, meet God face-to-face, and make a full declaration of his sin. Sooner or later, no matter how carefully we have hidden ourselves from God, every man and woman will have to come out from their hiding place, meet the all-holy God face-to-face, and make a full declaration of just where they stand in His presence.

I believe that God is putting the question of the text to every man and woman, to every Christian, and to everyone who is not a Christian. *Where art thou?* Where do you stand in regard to spiritual and eternal things? Where do you stand in regard to God, heaven, righteousness, Christ, and eternity? *Where art thou?*

Every wise man will be glad to face and answer that question. Every truly intelligent man desires to know just where he is. In business every wise businessman desires to know where he stands financially. In our country at this time of year, every careful businessman takes an inventory of his stock, totals his accounts, calculates his credits and debits, and determines his assets and liabilities. He wants to know where he stands. He may discover that he does not stand as well as he thought he did. He may find that he is in debt, when he hoped that his capital exceeded his liabilities. If that is true, he wants to know so he may conduct his business accordingly. Many a man has made a shipwreck of his business through unwillingness to face facts and find out where he stood.

Years ago, I knew a brilliant businessman, a man gifted along certain lines of business enterprise. But his affairs got into a tangled condition. His wise business friends came to him and advised him to go through his books and find out where he stood. They said to him, "If you are in bad shape, we will help you out."

But the man was too proud to take their advice; he was too proud to admit that his business was in a bad way, so he refused to look into it. He gritted his teeth, set his face like a flint, and tried to plunge through. But instead of plunging through, he plunged into utter financial ruin. Though he was an exceptionally brilliant man in some ways, he made such a complete financial shipwreck that he never got on his feet again. When he died, he did not have money enough to pay his funeral expenses, and I had to pay them out of my own pocket, simply because he was not willing to swallow his pride and face facts.

Many of you also are too proud to face the fact that you are morally and spiritually bankrupt, so you are going to grit your teeth, set your face like a flint, and plunge through. You will plunge into utter and eternal ruin.

Every man wants to know where he stands physically; he wants to know the condition of his lungs, his heart, his stomach, and his nerves. He may be worse off than he thinks he is; he may think his heart is sound when his heart is defective. But if that is the case, he wants to know it, because if he knows that his heart is defective, he will not subject it to the strain that he otherwise would. Many a man lies today in a premature grave who might have been doing good work on earth, because he was not willing to determine what his real condition was and act accordingly.

Every man at sea wishes to know the location of his vessel – its exact latitude and its exact longitude. I remember once in crossing the Atlantic Ocean some years ago, we had been sailing for days beneath clouds and through fog. We had been unable to take an observation by the sun and had been sailing by dead reckoning. One night I happened to be on deck, and suddenly there was a rift in the clouds just where the North Star appeared. Word was sent below to the commanding officer. The captain of the vessel hurried on deck and I remember how he fairly laid across the compass, and how carefully he took an observation by the North Star so we might know exactly where we were.

We are all sailing across a perilous sea toward an eternal port, and every truly intelligent man and woman will desire to know just where they are – their exact spiritual longitude and their exact spiritual latitude.

How shall we consider this great question?

Seriously

First of all, we should consider it seriously. It is not a question to trifle with. It is a singular fact that people who are intelligent and sensible about everything else, who would not think of trifling with the great financial questions of the day or with great social problems, when they come to this great question of eternity, will treat it as a joke. I remember one night in an American city, a little shoe-shiner on the street was blacking my boots, and I asked this shoe-shiner the question, "My boy, are you saved?" and the boy treated it as a joke. I was not surprised; that is what you would expect of a poor, illiterate, uneducated shoe-shiner on the street.

But it is not what you would expect of thinking men and thinking women, that when you come to these great eternal problems of God – eternity, salvation, heaven, and hell – that they would be treated as a joke. But these things are treated as a joke by some people. Any man or woman who trifles with questions like these plays the part of a fool. I don't care what your culture is, what your social position is, what your reputation is for scholarship. I don't hesitate to affirm that unless you have faced, or will face, this great question of your spiritual condition with the most profound earnestness and seriousness, you are playing the part of a fool.

Honestly

Secondly, we should consider this question honestly. There are many people in our day who are trying to deceive themselves, trying to deceive others, and trying to deceive God. There are many men who, in their inmost hearts know that they are wrong, yet are trying to persuade themselves that they are right, trying to persuade others that they are right, and trying to persuade God that they are right.

You cannot deceive God. It will do you no good to deceive anybody else, and it is complete folly to deceive yourself. The biggest fool on earth is the man who fools himself. Be honest. If you are lost, admit it; if you are on the road to hell, acknowledge it; if you are not a Christian, say so; if you are an enemy of God, face the facts; if you are a child of the devil, admit it. Be honest – honest with yourself, honest with your fellow man, and honest with God.

Thoroughly

In the third place, we should consider the question thoroughly. There are many people who are honest enough and serious enough as far as they go, but they don't follow through. They are superficial. They give these tremendous questions a few moments' thought, and then their weak minds grow weary, and they say, "I guess I am all right; I will take my chances."

> The biggest fool on earth is the man who fools himself.

You can't afford to guess on questions like these. We must have not probability, but absolute certainty. It will not satisfy me to hope I am saved; I must know that I am saved. It will not satisfy me to hope I am a child of God; I must know that I am a child of God. It will not satisfy me to hope that I am bound for heaven; I must know that I am bound for heaven. Do not lay these questions down until you have embraced them and know for an absolute certainty just where you stand.

Prayerfully

In the fourth place, you should consider these questions prayerfully. God tells us in His Word, and we know it from experience, that *the heart is deceitful above all things, and it is exceedingly corrupt* (Jeremiah 17:9). There is nothing that the human heart is so deceitful about as its moral and spiritual condition. Every man and woman by nature is very sharp-sighted to the faults of others and very blind to their own faults. What we need is to face this question in prayer. You will never know where you stand until God shows you. Not until we pray at least the substance of David's prayer: *Search me, O God, and know my heart: try me, and know my thoughts; and see if there be any wicked way in me* (Psalm 139:23-24), and God sheds the light of His Holy Spirit into our hearts and shows us ourselves as He sees us, will we ever know ourselves as we really are.

The great Scottish poet Burns never said a wiser thing than when he wrote:

> Oh, would some Power give us the gift,
> To see ourselves as others see us!
> It would from many a blunder free us,
> And foolish notion.[1]

But there is something better than to see ourselves as others see us, and that is to see ourselves as God sees us. Let us not leave until we see ourselves in the light of God's presence, as God sees us, and that will only happen in answer to definite and earnest prayer.

One morning in an American city I met the pastor of a church of which I had formerly been pastor. As we met, he said to me, "Brother Torrey, I had an awful experience this morning."

I said, "What was it, Brother Norris?"

"You know Mrs. So-and-so?" he said, mentioning a member of the church. "You know she is dying. She sent for me to come and see her this morning. I hurried to her home. The moment I opened the door and entered the room, she cried from her

---

1   Robert Burns, "To a Louse, On Seeing One on a Lady's Bonnet at Church" (Standard English translation from the Burns original), 1786.

bed, 'Oh, Brother Norris, I have been a professing Christian for forty years. I am now dying and have just found out in my dying hour that I was never saved at all.'"

The horror of it! To be a professing Christian for forty years and never realize until your life is at an end that you have never really been a Christian at all. Better to discover it then than in eternity, but better to understand it in the dawn of your professed Christian experience. Better to find it out now.

I do not doubt that in this great crowd there are many who have been professing Christians for years, but they were never saved. After we had left Liverpool, I read a letter in a paper edited by a clergyman in that city who was complaining about our meetings. In this letter, addressed to the public press, the writer said, "These men produced the impression that some of our church members are not saved." Well, that is the impression we tried to produce, for that is the truth of God. In the Church of England and in the Nonconformist bodies, you will find many who are unsaved.

Any hope founded on the Bible is a sure hope.

Scripturally

Once more we should consider this question scripturally according to the Bible. God has given to you and me only one safe chart and compass to guide us on our voyage through life toward eternity. That chart and compass is the Bible – the Book I hold in my hand. If you steer your course according to this book, you steer safely; if you steer your course according to your own feelings, according to the speculation of the petty philosopher or the theologian, according to anything but the clear declaration of the only Book of God, you steer your course toward shipwreck. Any hope that is not founded on the clear, unmistakable teaching of God's Word is absolutely worthless.

Any hope founded on the Bible is a sure hope; any hope that is not built upon the Bible is not worth anything.

In one of my pastorates, the heavenly Father had entrusted a young married couple with a sweet little child for a brief period. Then God, in His infinite wisdom, and wisdom in this case that was altogether incomprehensible, took that little child home to Himself. Their hearts were deeply touched, and in the hour of their sorrow, I went to call upon them. Taking advantage of their tenderness of heart, I pointed them to that Savior with whom their child was safely at home. And they professed to accept that Savior.

After some days and weeks had passed and the first keenness of the sorrow had gone, they drifted back into the world. I called upon them to speak with them. Only the wife was at home. I began by talking about the little child – and how safe and happy it was in the arms of Jesus. Of course, she gladly assented.

Then I turned it a little bit and said to her, "Do you expect to see your child again?"

"Oh," she said, "certainly; I have no doubt that I will see my child again."

I said, "Why do you expect to see your child again?"

She said, "Because the child is with Jesus, and I expect to be with Him when I die too."

I said, "Do you think you are saved?"

"Oh yes," she said, "I think I am saved."

I said, "Why do you think you are saved?"

"Because I feel so," she said.

I said, "Do you think you have eternal life?"

"Oh yes," she said, "I think I have eternal life."

I said, "Why do you think you have eternal life?"

"Because," she said, "I feel so."

I said, "Is that your only ground of hope?"

She said, "That is all."

I said, "Your hope is not worth anything." That seemed cruel, didn't it? But it was kind. I said, "Your hope is not worth anything. Can you put your finger on anything in the sure Word of God that proves you have everlasting life?"

"No," she said, "I cannot."

"Well, then," I said, "your hope is absolutely worthless."

Then she turned on me, which she had a perfect right to do. It is quite right to talk back to preachers – I believe in it – and she began to talk back. She said, "Do you expect to go to heaven when you die?"

I said, "Yes, I know I shall."

She said, "When you die, you expect to be with Christ?"

"Yes," I said, "I know I shall."

She said, "Do you think you have everlasting life?"

"Yes," I said, "I know I have."

She said, "Can you put your finger on anything in the Word of God that proves you have eternal life?"

I said, "Yes, thank God, John 3:36: *He that believeth on the Son hath eternal life.* Now, I know I believe in the Son of God, and on the sure ground of God's Word, I know I have everlasting life."

Can you put your finger upon anything in the Word of God that proves you are saved? If you can't, I advise you to find out if you are saved; if not, be saved right now. And if you are saved, find out something in God's Word that proves it.

Additional Questions

Are you saved or are you lost?
One thing more before I close, and that is a few suggestions that will help you in considering this question: *Where art thou?* Are you saved or are you lost? You are one or the other.

Unless you have been definitely saved by a definite acceptance of a definite Jesus, Jesus Christ, you are definitely lost. There are just two classes – lost sinners and saved sinners. To which class do you belong?

Are you on the road to heaven or the road to hell?
You are on one or the other. There are only two roads, as we see by the Scripture lesson which I present. The Lord Jesus tells us that there are two and only two roads – the broad road which leads to destruction and the narrow road that leads to life everlasting. Which road are you on? Are you on the road that leads up to God and heaven and glory, or are you on the road that leads down to Satan and sin and shame and hell?

Some years ago, an English sailor came into a mission in New York City, and as he left the mission not very much affected, a worker at the door put a little card into his hand. On this card were printed these words: "If I should die tonight, I would go to . . . ." The place was left blank, and underneath it was written, "Please fill out, and sign your name." The sailor, without even reading the card, put it in his pocket, went down to the ship to his bunk, and put that card on the edge of his bunk. On the journey, he was thrown from the rigging; this broke his leg. They took him down to his berth, and as he lay there day after day, that card stared him in the face. He looked at it one day: "If I should die tonight, I would go to . . . ."

"Well," he said, "if I filled that out honestly, I would have to write 'hell.' If I should die tonight, I would go to hell. But, I won't fill it out that way." Lying there in his berth, he took Jesus Christ and filled out the card: "If I should die tonight, I would go to heaven." He went on to England but came back to

> Unless you have been definitely saved by a definite acceptance of a definite Jesus Christ, you are definitely lost.

New York, walked into the mission, and handed in the card with his name signed to it.

Suppose you had such a card to fill out: "If I should die tonight, I would go to . . . ." What would your honest answer be?

Are you a child of God or a child of the devil?
We live in a day in which many superficial thinkers tell us that all men are the children of God. That is not the teaching of the Bible, and it is not the teaching of Jesus Christ. Jesus Christ says distinctly in John 8:44, talking to certain Jews, *Ye are of your father the devil.* And we are told in 1 John 3:10 that *in this the children of God are manifest, and the children of the devil.* And we are told distinctly in John 1:12 that *as many as received him, to them gave he the right to* **become** *children of God.* Children of God, or children of the devil. Every one of us is either one or the other. Which are you?

When I was speaking more than a year ago in the city of Ballarat in Australia, there sat a long line of educated Chinese men in the meeting listening to the sermon. I was preaching on the same text. I came to the point I have come to now, and I said to myself, "I guess I will leave that out; that may offend somebody without doing any good." But somehow God would not let me leave it out, so I put it in and declared the whole counsel of God.

> Children of God, or children of the devil. Every one of us is either one or the other.

The next night when I gave the invitation, among the others who came to the front was almost the entire line of educated Chinese men. When they got up to give their testimony, one of them said, "The reason I came tonight and took Christ was that I was here last night and heard Dr. Torrey say that everyone was either a child of God or a child of the devil. I knew I was not a child of God, and therefore I knew I must be a child of the devil. I made up my mind I would be a child of the devil no longer, and therefore I have come forward tonight to take Jesus Christ." I hope some of you will have as much sense as that educated Chinese man.

What kind of Christian are you?

Are you a mere formal Christian, or are you a real Christian? You know there are two kinds. Are you one of these men or women who call themselves Christians, who go to the house of God on Sunday, who go to Communion, and perhaps teach a Bible class or a Sunday school class, but run around to the theater, a card party, dances, and all the frivolity and foolishness of the world the rest of the week? Are you one of the Christians who is trying to hold on to Jesus Christ with one hand and the world with the other? Or are you a real Christian who has renounced the world with your whole heart and given yourself to Jesus Christ with all your heart, a Christian who can sing, "I surrender all" and mean it? *Where art thou?* What kind of a Christian are you?

Are you for Christ or are you against Him?

You know you are either one or the other, for He says so. We read in Matthew 12:30 in the words of Jesus Himself: *He that is not with me is against me.* Everyone is either with Jesus wholeheartedly, confessedly, and openly, or else they are against Jesus. Which are you? For Christ or against Him?

In my first pastorate, year after year for a number of years there came an outpouring of God's Spirit. In the second or third of these gracious outpourings of His Spirit, a great many of the leading businessmen of the place were converted. It was a small place, but one of the leading businessmen would not take a stand. He was one of the most exemplary men in the community – most amiable, attractive, upright, a constant attendee at church, a member of my Bible class, and a member of my choir, but he was one of those men who wanted to please both sides. He was identified with friends in business, in the Masonic lodge, and elsewhere who were not out-and-out Christians, and he was afraid that he would alienate them if he came out honestly for Christ.

So the weeks passed by. After the service one Sunday morning, as he was leaving my Bible class on the choir platform, he passed by the superintendent of the Sunday school, who was an intimate friend. They had been in the Civil War together. As he passed by this intimate friend, he turned to him and said, "George?"

"Well, what is it, Porter?" said the other, calling him by his first name.

He said, "George, when are you going to take a stand?"

He said, "Ring the bell."

Promptly the superintendent stepped up to the bell and rang it, and the congregation going out of the building turned around in surprise, wondering what was going to happen. George stepped to the front of the platform. In this community everybody knew everybody else by their first name, so they were all curious. George said, "Friends, I have heard it said time and again during these meetings that a man must either be for Jesus Christ or against Him. I want you all to know that from this time on, Em (his wife) and I are for Christ."

He decided for the whole family, and he truly did, in fact, for when they stood before the platform to receive the right hand of fellowship into the church, he stood there with his wife, his father-in-law, his brother-in-law, and his sister-in-law – every member of the family that was not already in the fold.

There are many of you whose sympathies for years have been with the church of Jesus Christ, but you have never been man enough or woman enough to take an open stand. Take it now. Say, "As for me and my house, we are for Christ." *Where art thou?* Put the question to yourself. *Where art thou?*

There is one reason that makes it exceedingly important for you to face this question, and that is the fact that where you are now will in all likelihood determine where you shall spend eternity.

A story is told of Dr. Forbes Winslow, the elder of London, the eminent pathologist in diseases of the mind. A young French nobleman came to London with letters of introduction from leading Frenchmen, including one from Napoleon III who was at that time emperor. These letters introduced him to Dr. Forbes Winslow and solicited Winslow's best offices for the young man. He presented his letters, and Dr. Winslow said, "What is your trouble?"

He said, "Dr. Winslow, I cannot sleep; I have not had a good night's sleep for two years, and unless something is done for me I shall go insane."

Dr. Winslow said, "Why can't you sleep?"

"Well," said the young man, "I can't tell you."

Dr. Winslow said, "Have you lost any money?"

"No," he said, "I have lost no money."

"Have you lost friends?"

"No, I have lost no friends recently."

"Have you suffered in honor or reputation?"

"Not that I know of."

"Well then," said the doctor, "why can't you sleep?"

The young man said, "I would rather not tell you."

"Well," said Dr. Winslow, "if you don't tell me, I can't help you."

"Well," he said, "if I must tell you, I will. I am an infidel. My father was an infidel before me, and yet in spite of the fact that I am an infidel and my father was an infidel, every night when I lie down to sleep, I am confronted with the question of eternity and where I shall spend it. All night that question rings in my ears: *Eternity, where shall I spend it?* If I succeed in getting to sleep, my dreams are worse than my waking hours, and I wake from my sleep again."

Dr. Winslow said, "I can't do anything for you."

"What?" said the young Frenchman. "Have I come all the way over here from Paris for you to treat me but have you dash my hopes to the ground? Do you mean to tell me that my case is hopeless?"

Dr. Winslow repeated, "I can do nothing for you, but I can tell you a Physician who can," and he walked across his study, took up his Bible from the center of the table, and opened it to Isaiah 53:5-6. He read: *He was wounded for our transgressions, he was bruised for our iniquities: the chastisement of our peace was upon him; and with his stripes we are healed. All we like sheep have gone astray; we have turned every one to his own way; and the LORD hath laid on him the iniquity of us all.*

And then, looking at the Frenchman, he said, "That is the only Physician in the world that can help you."

There was a curl of scorn upon the Frenchman's lips. He said, "Dr. Winslow, do you mean to tell me that you, an eminent scientist, believe in that worn-out superstition of the Bible and Christianity?"

"Yes," said Dr. Winslow, "I believe the Bible; I believe in Jesus Christ; and believing in the Bible and believing in Jesus Christ has saved me from what you are today."

The young fellow stopped and thought; then he said, "Dr. Winslow, if I am an honest man, I ought at least to be willing to consider it, shouldn't I?"

"Yes, sir."

"Well," he said, "will you explain it to me?"

And the eminent physician became a physician of souls; he sat down with his open Bible and for several consecutive days showed the young Frenchman the way of life. The Frenchman saw Christ as his divine, atoning Savior and put his trust in Him; he went back to Paris with peace of mind to sleep at night. He had solved the great question of eternity and where he would spend it, for he would spend it with Christ in glory.

Where will you spend eternity? Where you will spend eternity very likely will depend upon where you are right now.

Chapter 2

The Appalling Sin of
Unbelief in Jesus Christ

He that believeth not is condemned already,
because he hath not believed in the name of the
only begotten Son of God. (John 3:18)

The failure to put faith in Jesus Christ is not a mere misfortune; it is a sin, a grievous sin, an appalling sin, a damning sin. *He that believeth not is condemned already, because he hath not believed in the name of the only begotten Son of God* (John 3:18). Men will tell you very lightly and laughingly, "I do not believe in Jesus Christ." Indeed, men will tell you with an airy toss of the head, as if it were something they were quite proud of, "I do not believe in Jesus Christ." Few men are so foolish and so blind, or so utterly depraved, as to tell you laughingly or proudly, "I am a murderer," or "I am an adulterer," or "I am a habitual liar." Yet none of these is a sadder or darker confession than "I am an unbeliever in Jesus Christ."

Believing or not believing in Jesus Christ is largely a matter of the will and not altogether a matter of intellectual conviction.

There are those who imagine it is wholly a matter of intellectual conviction whether one believes or does not believe in Jesus Christ. The one who thinks so is a very superficial thinker. There are very few people in this audience who don't have sufficient evidence that Jesus is the Son of God and the Savior of those who believe in Him, if they were only willing to yield themselves to the evidence. The will plays a large part in what a man believes politically, and the will plays a still larger part in believing in Jesus Christ. The people who believe in Jesus Christ believe in Him because they will to yield to the truth and to believe in Him who is so clearly and so abundantly proven to be God's Son.

Those who do not believe in Jesus Christ do not believe in Him because, for the love of sin or some other reason, they will not yield to the truth and accept Him as Savior and Lord, who is so abundantly proven to be the Son of God. Most of you who do not believe in Jesus Christ know that this is true. You know that your refusal to accept Jesus Christ is not because you have grave reasons for believing that Jesus Christ is not what He claims to be. You know it is because you do not want to accept Him, surrender your life to Him, and confess Him. Now, this is a great sin. This sin is a greater sin than any you can commit against any fellow man by lying to him, stealing from him, or killing him. It is greater than falsehood, theft, or murder. If you will give me your honest attention, I will prove to you that this is so. Don't try to get away from the truth by getting out of the house, whispering to someone, refusing to listen, or laughing contemptuously. If you do, you will do it to your own eternal ruin. If I am right in this matter, and if the Bible is right, it is of infinite importance that you know it; so consider carefully and candidly.

> The people who believe in Jesus Christ believe in Him because they will to yield to the truth.

Because of Who Jesus Christ Is

Unbelief in Jesus Christ is an appalling sin because of who Jesus Christ is and the dignity of His person. Jesus Christ is the Son of God, the only begotten Son of God. He is the Son of God in a sense that no other person is the Son of God. He is the radiance of His Father's glory and the express image of His person (Hebrews 1:3). *In him dwelleth all the fulness of the Godhead bodily* (Colossians 2:9). He is the One of whom God the Father said, *Let all the angels of God worship him* (Hebrews 1:6). Of Him the Father says *that all men should honour the Son, even as they honour the Father* (John 5:23). A dignity attaches to the person of Jesus Christ that attaches to no angel or archangel or to none of the principalities or powers in the heavenly places. His is the name that is above every name; *that at the name of Jesus every knee should bow, . . . and that every tongue should confess that Jesus Christ is Lord* (Philippians 2:10-11).

An injury done to Jesus Christ is then a sin of vastly greater magnitude than a sin done to man. A horse, a cow, or a mule has rights, but the rights of a horse, or a cow, or a mule are minuscule when compared to the rights of a man. The law recognizes the rights of a mule, but the willful killing of a mule is not regarded as seriously as the willful putting out of a man's eye. But the rights of a man, even of the purest, noblest, greatest of men, pale into infinitesimal insignificance before the rights of that infinite Being whom we call God, and His infinite Son, Jesus Christ. To realize the enormity of a sin committed against Jesus Christ, we must strive to get some adequate conception of the dignity and majesty of His person. When we do, we see that robbing this infinitely glorious person by our unbelief of that honor which is His due is a sin that in comparison, the rankest injustice or enormity committed against man is as nothing.

What was it that struck conviction in the hearts of three thousand men on the day of Pentecost and made them cry out in agony, *Men and brethren, what shall we do?* (Acts 2:37). It was this – Peter, filled with the Spirit, told them who Jesus was. He said, *Let all the house of Israel therefore know assuredly, that God hath made him both Lord and Christ, this Jesus whom ye crucified* (Acts 2:36). Their eyes were opened at last to see the glory, the dignity, and the majesty of the person of Him whom they had so outrageously wronged. All the sins of their lifetime were instantly seen to be nothing in comparison with this sin.

And if you will permit God to open your eyes to see who Jesus is, to see the infinite dignity, glory, and majesty of His divine person, you will see that every conceivable wrong done to any mere man is nothing compared to the wrong done to this magnificent person. You may refuse to let God open your eyes to the infinite glory of Jesus; you may say, I don't see that He is essentially greater than other men or that His rights are more sacred than those of Longfellow, Lincoln, Washington, or my next-door neighbor, but the day will come when you will have to see. The day will come when the full glory of Jesus will be unveiled to the whole universe, and in that day, if you will not repent now and receive pardon for your awful sin of unbelief in this glorious Son of God, you will be overwhelmed with eternal shame. You will cry for the rocks and the hills to fall upon you and hide you from the wrath of Him who sits on the throne of the universe and the wrath of the Lamb. You will wish to rush from the presence of that heavenly glory into eternal darkness to get away from the presence of Him whom you have so grievously wronged. On and on and on you will wish to flee – away, away, away, eternally away from the outraged Son of God.

One night God gave me such a vision of the glory of Jesus Christ that I saw the appalling nature of sin against Him, this infinitely glorious One. You may not have had such a vision, nor do you need to have it, for you know what God's own testimony regarding Jesus is. That testimony is in His Book. In the light of that testimony, you may know that the most grievous wrong against man – theft, adultery, murder – is as nothing. It is for this reason that our text says, He who believes in Him is not condemned; he who does not believe is condemned already, *because he hath not believed in the name of the only begotten Son of God.*

Because Faith Is Supreme

Unbelief in Jesus Christ is an appalling sin not only because of the dignity of Christ's person, but also because faith is the supreme thing that is His due. Jesus is worthy of many things. He is worthy of our admiration; He is worthy of our attention; He is worthy of our obedience; He is worthy of our service; He is worthy of our testimony; He is worthy of our love. All these things are His due. To not give Him these things is to rob Him of His due, to rob a Being of infinite importance of His due.

> He who believes in Him is not condemned; he who does not believe is condemned already.

But first, underlying all else, and above all else, Jesus Christ is worthy of faith; man's confidence is due to Jesus Christ. He is infinitely worthy of the surrender to Himself of the confidence of our intellects, our feelings, and our wills. It is due to Him to say, "Lord Jesus, infinite Son of God, I surrender my mind's complete faith, the complete confidence of my heart and my will." He is worthy of that – His first great right. If you refuse to do that, and many of you have refused to do it week after week, month after month, and year after year, you have robbed Jesus Christ. You have robbed this glorious divine person of His first and greatest right; you have robbed a divine person of His supreme due. So it is written in our text: *He that believeth not is condemned already, because he hath not believed in the name of the only begotten Son of God.*

Because He Is the Incarnation of God

Unbelief in Jesus Christ is an appalling sin because Jesus Christ is the incarnation of all the infinite moral perfections of God's own being. God is light, and in him is no darkness at all (1 John 1:5). This infinite, absolute light, which is God, this infinite holiness and love and truth, is incarnate in Jesus Christ, and the refusal to accept Him is the refusal of light and the choice of darkness.

Nothing more clearly proves what a man is at heart than what he chooses and rejects.

It is the clearest possible proof that the one who rejects Him loves darkness rather than light. Nothing more clearly proves what a man is at heart than what he chooses and what he rejects. A man who chooses foul books, foul pictures, and foul friends is a foul man no matter what his claims may be. A man who rejects the good, the pure, and the true is bad, impure, and false. To reject Christ is to reject the infinite light of God; this reveals a heart that is so corrupt that it loves darkness rather than light. So it is written in our text: *He that believeth not is condemned already, because he hath not believed in the name of the only begotten Son of God. And this is the condemnation, that light is come into the world, and men loved darkness rather than light, because their deeds were evil* (John 3:18-19). Unbelief in Jesus Christ is indeed an appalling sin.

Because Unbelief Tramples the Love and Mercy of God

Unbelief in Jesus Christ is an appalling sin because it is trampling underfoot the infinite love and mercy of God. Jesus Christ is the supreme expression of God's love and mercy to sinners. *For God so loved the world, that he gave his only begotten Son, that whosoever believeth on him should not perish, but have eternal life* (John 3:16). We have all broken God's holy laws and thus have brought the wrath of the Holy One upon ourselves, but God still loves us; instead of banishing us forever from His presence into the outer darkness where there is only agony and despair, He has provided a way of salvation for us. He provided that way at infinite cost to Himself. His saving love had no limit; it stopped at no sacrifice; He gave His best, His only begotten Son, to redeem us.

All that we need to do to be saved is to believe in that Son and to put our trust in the pardoning mercy and love of God thus revealed. But instead of believing, and thereby obtaining eternal life, what are many of you doing? You are not believing; you are rejecting this love and its provision. You are despising and trampling underfoot the salvation that God has so dearly purchased and offered to you. You are scorning and insulting infinite love and mercy. That is what unbelief in Jesus Christ is; it is scorn and contempt and insult to infinite, pardoning love.

Every man and woman, young and old, who does not render the faith of their whole being to Jesus Christ and does not receive Him as the Son of God, their Lord and Savior, is guilty of scorning and insulting the infinite, pardoning love of God. Some of you go even beyond that; you try to make yourselves believe that Jesus is not the Son of God. You try to make yourselves believe that there is no need of an atonement; you laugh at the sacrifice the loving Father has made so that you, His guilty, hell-deserving subjects, might be saved. Yes, there are people who do this. Thousands in this city do it. One sometimes almost wonders why the outraged love of God does not turn to blazing wrath, and why God does not blast the world of Christ-rejecting men with the breath of His mouth. Unbelief in Jesus Christ is an appalling sin because it is scorn and contempt for infinite love.

There are other reasons why unbelief in Jesus Christ is an appalling sin, but these are four tremendous reasons, and they are enough: First, because of the infinite dignity of His person. Second, because that faith is His supreme due, so not to give it is to rob a divine person of His supreme right. Third, because Jesus Christ is the incarnation of all the infinite moral perfections of God's own being. Fourth, because it is trampling underfoot the infinite love and mercy of God.

Clearly, unbelief in Jesus Christ is an appalling sin. Theft is a gross sin; adultery is worse; murder is shocking; but when our eyes are opened, we see that all these are as nothing compared to the violation of the dignity and majesty of the person of Jesus Christ, the only begotten Son of God, by our unbelief. How God must abhor the sin of unbelief! How the holy angels in heaven must abhor the sin of unbelief! How all holy men and women must abhor the sin of unbelief!

And of this awful, appalling sin, many of you are guilty. Not only the gross infidel and the refined skeptic are guilty of this sin, but also everyone who holds back from giving to Jesus the wholehearted surrender of his whole self – mind, affections, and will. All who fail to gladly welcome Him as Savior and Lord are guilty of this appalling sin today. Don't some of you cry out as did the three thousand at Pentecost, *What shall we do?* It is because of the hardness of your hearts. Soften those hearts of stone; publicly confess your awful sin now; forsake it now. Don't rest another day under such awful guilt. We see why it is that unbelief leads to eternal doom. We see why it is that no matter how many good things a man may do, if he refuses to believe in Jesus Christ, he must forever perish. Give up your awful unbelief in Jesus Christ and accept Him now.

Chapter 3

Hell: Its Certainty, What It Is, and How to Escape It

And if thy right eye causeth thee to stumble,
pluck it out, and cast it from thee: for it is profit-
able for thee that one of thy members should
perish, and not thy whole body be cast into hell.
(Matthew 5:29)

My subject in this chapter is hell: its certainty, what it is, and how to escape it. If I were to choose my own subject, I certainly would never choose this. I always address it with reluctance and pain. It is an awful subject, but a minister of God has no right to choose his own subjects. He must go to God for them, and I am confident that God wishes me to address this awful subject.

I wish that I could believe that there was no hell; that is, I wish that I could believe that all men would come to repentance and accept Christ, and that hell would be unnecessary. Of course, if men persist in sin and in the rejection of Christ, God's glorious Son, I cannot help but recognize that it is right that there should be a hell and that hell should continue as long as men persist in their sin and rejection of Christ. If men will choose sin, it is for the good of the universe and the glory of God that there should be a hell to confine them in, but I wish with all my heart that all men would repent and thus render hell unnecessary, as far as the human race is concerned. I do not wish to believe it if it is not true, but I would rather believe and preach unpleasant truth than to believe and preach pleasant error.

And as awful as the thought is, I have been driven to the conclusion that there is a hell. I once honestly believed and taught that all men, even the devil, would ultimately come to repentance so that hell would cease to be. But I came to the conclusion that I could not honestly reconcile this position with the teaching of Christ and the apostles. I was driven to this alternative – that I must either give up my Bible or give up my eternal hope. I could not give up the Bible. I had become thoroughly convinced that the Bible, beyond a doubt, was the very Word of God. I could not in honesty twist and distort the Scriptures to make them agree with what I wanted to believe.

> I know that if a man stands on the teaching of Christ he will be called narrow. But I have no desire to be any broader than Jesus Christ.

As an honest man, there was only one thing left for me to do, and that was to give up my opinion that all men would ultimately come to repentance and be saved. I know perfectly well that if a man stands squarely on the teaching of Christ and the apostles and declares it without fear, he will be called narrow, harsh, and cruel. But as to being narrow, I have no desire to be any broader than Jesus Christ; as to being cruel, is it cruel to tell men the truth? Isn't it the kindest thing that one can do to declare the whole counsel of God and to point out to men the full measure of their danger?

Suppose that I'm walking down a railway track, knowing that

far behind me there's a train coming that is loaded with happy vacationers – men, women, and children full of joy and glee. I come to a place where I had assumed there was a bridge across the chasm, but to my horror, I find that the bridge is down. I say to myself, "I must go back at once and stop that oncoming train. I hurry back and do my best to stop the train. I interrupt the people with the awful announcement that the bridge is down, and they are in peril of a frightful disaster. I spoil the merriment of the evening, and I banish the bright thoughts from their minds and replace them with horrid thoughts of imminent disaster. Would that be cruel? No, wouldn't it be the kindest thing that I could do?

Suppose, on the other hand, that when I had found the bridge down, I had said, "These people are so happy, I cannot bear to disturb their night's lightheartedness and gaiety. That would be too cruel. Instead, I will sit down here and wait until the train comes." So I sit down while the train comes rushing on, unaware of the danger, and plunges into that awful abyss. Soon the despairing shrieks and groans of the wounded and mangled are rising as those vacationers crawl out from among the corpses of the dead. Would that be kind? No, wouldn't it be the cruelest thing that I could do?

In my country, if I acted that way, I would be arrested for manslaughter. I have been down the track. I had supposed that there was a bridge across the chasm. I have found that the bridge is down. I have discovered that many of you who are now full of gaiety and joy are rushing, unwarned of the awful fate that awaits you. I have come back up the track to warn you. I may ruin for the time your joyfulness and merriment, but by God's grace, I will save you from the awful doom. Is that cruel? No, isn't it the kindest thing that I can do? I would much rather be called cruel for being kind than be called kind for being cruel. The cruelest man on earth is the man who believes the stern things we are told in the Word of God about the future penalties of sin, but refrains from declaring them because they are unpopular.

I will not give you my own speculations about the future destiny of the unrepentant. My speculations would be worth as much as those of other men and no more. They would be worth practically nothing at all. Man's speculations on such a subject are without any value. God knows; we don't. But God has been pleased to tell us much of what He knows about it. Let us listen to Him. One ounce of God's revelation about the future is worth a hundred tons of man's speculation. One hears on every side: "I think so-and-so about the future life." What difference does it make what you think? The question is, What does God say?

> I will not give you my own speculations about the future destiny of the unrepentant. God knows; we don't.

You will find my text in Matthew 5:29: *And if thy right eye causeth thee to stumble, pluck it out, and cast it from thee: for it is profitable for thee that one of thy members should perish, and not thy whole body be cast into hell.* You will notice I take my text from the Sermon on the Mount. I take it from the Sermon on the Mount for two reasons: first, because it exactly suits my purpose; second, because a great many men in our day say they believe in the Sermon on the Mount though they do not believe in the whole Bible. So, I have taken my text from that part of the Bible that you all say you believe. And you will notice I have taken it from the American Standard Version. I have done that for two reasons. First, because the American Standard Version is a more accurate translation in this instance than the Authorized Version; and second, because a great many men say that the American Standard Version has done away with hell. Well, there seems to be plenty of it left in the text. But, you say, that text is highly figurative. Very well, let it go at that.

It at least means this much – almost anything is better than going to hell, and that is my chief proposition at this moment. Almost anything is better than going to hell.

What I have to say will come under three headings: first, the certainty of hell; second, the character of hell; and third, how to escape hell.

The Certainty of Hell

It is certain that there is a hell. Some people will tell you that all the scholarly ministers and clergymen have denied the orthodox hell. That simply is not so. That kind of argument is a favorite argument with men who know that they have a weak case and try to bolster up a weak case by strong assertion. It is true beyond a doubt that some scholarly ministers have denied the orthodox hell, but they never doubt it for reasons of Greek or New Testament scholarship. They refute it for purely sentimental and speculative reasons. No man can go to the New Testament to discover what it really teaches, not to see how he can twist it into conformity with the speculations that he wishes to believe, and not find hell in the New Testament.

But suppose it were true. Suppose that every scholarly minister had given up believing in the orthodox hell; it would not prove anything. Everybody who is familiar with the history of the world and the history of the church knows that time after time the scholars have previously quit believing in doctrines that in the final outcome proved to be true.

There were no scholars in Noah's day except Noah who believed there would be a flood, but the flood came just the same. There were no scholars in Lot's day except Lot who believed that God would destroy Sodom and Gomorrah, but He did. Jeremiah and one friend were the only leading men in all Jerusalem who believed what Jeremiah taught about the coming destruction of Jerusalem under Nebuchadnezzar, but history outside the Bible as well as history inside the Bible tells us that it came true to the very letter, though no scholars believed it. Every leading school of theology in the days of Jesus Christ, the Pharisees, the Sadducees, the Herodians, and the Essenes scoffed at Jesus Christ's prediction about the coming judgment of God upon Jerusalem, but secular history tells us that in spite of the dissent of all the scholars, it came true just as Jesus Christ predicted.

There was not a university in the world and scarcely a leading scholar in the days of Martin Luther and John Huss that had not denied faith in the doctrine of justification by faith, until Huss and Luther and their colleagues came. They had to establish a new university to stand for the truth of God. But today we know that Martin Luther was right, and every university of Germany, France, England, and Scotland was wrong. So, if it were true that every scholarly preacher on earth had quit believing in the doctrine of the orthodox hell, it would not prove anything.

I say that hell is certain. Why? First, because Jesus Christ said so, and the apostles said so, and God said so. If you want the words of Jesus Christ, turn to Matthew 25:41: *Then shall he say also unto them on the left hand, Depart from me, ye cursed, into everlasting fire, prepared for the devil and his angels.* Read the words of Paul the apostle: *The Lord Jesus shall be revealed from heaven with his mighty angels, in flaming fire taking vengeance on them that know not God, and that obey not the gospel of our Lord Jesus Christ: who shall be punished with everlasting destruction from the presence of the Lord, and from the glory of his power* (2 Thessalonians 1:7-9).

If you want the words of the apostle John, turn to Revelation 20:15: *If any was not found written in the book of life, he was cast into the lake of fire.* Then read the words of the apostle Peter: *For if God spared not angels when they sinned, but cast them down to hell, and committed them to pits of darkness, to be reserved unto judgment; the Lord knoweth how to deliver the godly out of temptation, and to keep the unrighteous under punishment unto the day of judgment* (2 Peter 2:4, 9).

If you want the words of the apostle Jude, turn to Jude 1:14-15: *The Lord came with ten thousands of his holy ones, to execute judgment upon all, and to convict all the ungodly of all their works of ungodliness which they have ungodly wrought, and of all the hard things which ungodly sinners have spoken against him.*

Jesus Himself spoke of hell. After He had died and gone down into the abode of the dead, after He had risen again and ascended unto the right hand of His Father, He said, *But for the fearful, and unbelieving, and abominable, and murderers, and fornicators, and sorcerers, and idolaters, and all liars, their part shall be in the lake that burneth with fire and brimstone; which is the second death* (Revelation 21:8).

I say that hell is certain because Jesus Christ and the apostles say so, because God says so through them. The only thing countering it is the speculation of the theologians and the dreams of poets. The words of Christ have stood the test of eighteen centuries and always proved true in the final outcome every time. No school of theological speculation has ever stood the test of even eighteen years, and when I have Christ on one side and speculative theologians on the other, it doesn't take me long to decide which to believe.

In the second place, I say that hell is certain because experience, observation, and common sense prove that there is a hell. One of the most certain facts of every man's experience is that where there is sin, there must be suffering. We all know that. The second certain fact of observation is that the longer a man continues in sin, the deeper he sinks into it and into the ruin, shame, agony, and despair that are the outcomes of all sin.

There are hundreds and thousands of people in your city in a very practical hell, and the hell is getting worse every day. You may not know how to reconcile what these people suffer with the doctrine that God is love, but no intelligent man gives up obvious facts because he cannot explain the philosophy of them, and this is an obvious fact. Now, if this process continues, men sink ever deeper and deeper into ruin, shame, and despair.

When the time of possible repentance has passed, and it will be passed sometime, what is left but an everlasting hell? The only alternative is the dreams of poets and the speculations of would-be philosophers. But the speculations of philosophers have proved an *ignis fatuus* (something deceptive) from the very dawn of history. When on the one hand I have the teaching of observation, experience, and common sense, and on the other hand I only have the speculations of philosophers and the dreams of poets, it doesn't take me long to decide which to believe. But when, in addition to the teaching of observation, experience, and common sense in its conflict with the speculations of cloistered theologians, we have the sure teaching of the Word of God, the case is settled. There is a hell.

When we have the sure teaching of the Word of God, the case is settled.

It is more certain that there is a hell than that when you lie down to sleep tonight, you will wake again tomorrow morning. You probably will, but you may not. However, it is certain that there is a hell. The next time you buy a skillfully written book or hear an eloquent lecturer and pay a shilling or two shillings or four shillings to have some man prove to you that there is no hell, you are paying to be made a fool of. There is a hell.

The Characteristics of Hell

Suffering

First, hell is a place of extreme bodily suffering. That is plain from the teaching of the New Testament. The most common words to express the doom of the unrepentant are *death* and *destruction*. What do *death* and *destruction* mean? God has taken pains to define His terms. His definition of *destruction* is in Revelation 17:8 as compared with Revelation 19:20 and 20:10. In Revelation 17:8, we are told that the beast goes into *perdition*. The word there translated *perdition* is the same word which is translated *destruction* elsewhere and should be so translated here, or it should be translated differently in the other passages.

Now, if you can find where the beast goes, you have God's own definition of *perdition* or *destruction*. Revelation 19:20 says that the beast and the false prophet were *cast alive into the lake of fire that burneth with brimstone*. Then in Revelation 20:10, you are told that a thousand years later, the devil also is *cast into the lake of fire and brimstone, where are also the beast and the false prophet; and they shall be tormented day and night for ever and ever*. By God's own definition, perdition or destruction is a place in a lake of torment forever and ever.

Now let us look at God's definition of *death*. You will find it in Revelation 21:8: *The fearful, and unbelieving, and abominable, and murderers, and fornicators, and sorcerers, and idolaters, and all liars, their part shall be in the lake that burneth with fire and brimstone: which is the second death.*

God's definition of *death* is a portion *in the lake that burneth with fire and brimstone*, just the same as His definition of *perdition*.

"Oh," but somebody says," that is all highly figurative."

Very well. I don't care to contend that, but remember that God's figures stand for facts. Some people will say it is figurative when they come to something unwelcome in the Bible and imagine that they have done away with it altogether. You have not done away with it by calling it figurative. What does the figure mean? God is no liar, and God's figures never overstate the facts; it means at least this much: bodily suffering of the most intense kind.

Remember furthermore, in the next life we do not exist as disembodied spirits. All this theory so common today of the immortality of the soul independent of the body, where we float around as bodiless spirits, is Platonic philosophy and not New Testament teaching. According to the Bible, in the world to come the redeemed spirit has a body – not this same body but a radically different body – the perfect counterpart of the redeemed spirit that inhabits it and is a partaker in all its blessedness.

On the other hand, the lost spirit also has a body – not this same body but the perfect counterpart of the lost spirit that inhabits it and is a partaker with it in all its misery. Even in the present life, inward spiritual sin causes outward bodily pain.

How many men are suffering the most acute bodily pain because of inward sin! I once went to a hospital where there were more than twelve hundred people suffering the worst bodily pain, and the physician in charge told me that every one of them was brought there because of one specific sin. Hell is the hospital of the incurables of the universe, where men exist in excruciating and perpetual pain.

Memory and Remorse

But the physical pain is the least significant feature of hell. Hell is a place of memory and remorse. Remember the picture Christ has given us of the rich man in hell, when Abraham said to the rich man, *Remember* (Luke 16:25). The rich man had not taken much that he had on earth with him, but he had taken one thing: he had taken his memories.

You who continue in sin and spend eternity in hell, you won't take much with you that you own, but you will take one thing: you will take your memories. You men will remember the women whose lives you have blasted and ruined, and you women will remember the lives squandered in frivolousness, fashion, and foolishness, when you might have been living for God. You will remember the Christ that you rejected and the opportunities for salvation that you despised. There is no torment known to men like the torment of an accusing memories.

I have seen strong men weeping like children in my Chicago office. What was the problem? Memories. I have seen one of the strongest, brainiest men I ever knew throw himself on the floor of my office and roll and sob and groan and wail. What was the problem? Memories. I have had people hurry up to me at the close of a service with pale cheeks, drawn lips, and haunted eyes, and beg for a private conversation. What was the problem? Memories. You will take your memories with you, and the memory and the conscience that are not at peace in this life through the atoning blood of Christ and the pardoning grace of God will never be at peace. Hell is the place where men remember and suffer.

> There is no torment known to men like the torment of an accusing memories.

One day Mr. Moody asked me to go out riding, and after we had ridden a little ways, he drove into a cornfield, went out to the middle of the lot, and then he said, "This is where it happened."

I said, "This is where what happened?"

He said, "Don't you remember the last time I was in Chicago that I told you a certain story, and you said the next time you came to Northfield, you wanted me to show you just where it happened? This is where it happened."

What was the story?

When Mr. Moody was a mere lad, one day he was hoeing corn – maize, as you call it – across a field with an elderly man. Suddenly the man stopped hoeing and commenced hitting a stone with the hoe. Mr. Moody looked at him. The tears were rolling down his cheeks, and he said, "Dwight, when I was a lad like you, I left home to make a living for myself." His house was up on the hill; Mr. Moody pointed to the house as the man spoke. "As I came out of the front gate yonder, my mother handed me a Testament and said, 'My boy, *Seek ye first his kingdom, and his righteousness; and all these things shall be added unto you*'" (Matthew 6:33).

The man said, "I went to the next town. I went to church on Sunday. The minister got up to preach, and he announced his text to be Matthew 6:33. He looked right down at me, pointed his finger at me, and said, 'Young man, *Seek ye first his kingdom, and his righteousness; and all these things shall be added unto you.*' I went out of the church; I had an awful struggle; it seemed as if the minister were talking to me. I said no, I will get fixed in life first, and then I will become a Christian. But I found no work there. I went to another town, and I found employment. I went to church, as was my custom, Sunday after Sunday. After I had been going some Sundays, the minister stood up in the pulpit and announced his text. It was Matthew 6:33. *Seek ye first his kingdom, and his righteousness; and all these things shall be added unto you.*"

Then the man said, "Dwight, he seemed to look right at me and point his finger right at me, and say, 'Young man, *Seek ye first his kingdom, and his righteousness; and all these things shall be added unto you.*' I got up and went out of church. I went to the cemetery behind the church and sat down on a tombstone. I had an awful fight, but at last I said, 'No, I will not become a Christian until I get settled in life.'

"Dwight," he said, "from that day to this, the Spirit of God has left me, and I have never had the slightest inclination to become a Christian."

Mr. Moody said, "I did not understand it then. I was not a Christian myself. I went to Boston where I was converted. Then I understood. I wrote to my mother and asked her what had become of that man."

She wrote to me: "Dwight, he has gone insane, and they have taken him to the Brattleboro Insane Asylum."

Mr. Moody said, "I went home to Brattleboro and called on him there. He was in his cell, and as I went in, he glared at me, pointed his finger at me, and said, 'Young man, *Seek ye first his kingdom, and his righteousness*,' but I could do nothing with him.

"I went back to Boston, but after some time I came home again. I said to my mother, 'Where is Mr. So-and-so now?'"

"Oh!" she said, "he is home, but he is a helpless imbecile."

"I went up to his house. There he sat rocking back and forth in a rocking chair, a white-haired man. And as I went into the room, he pointed his finger at me and said, 'Young man, *Seek ye first his kingdom, and his righteousness*.' He was gone crazy with memory."

Hell is the madhouse of the universe where men and women remember.

Tormenting Desire

Hell is a place of insatiable and tormenting desire. Remember what Jesus tells us of Dives, the rich man in hell. The rich man said, *Send Lazarus, that he may dip the tip of his finger in water, and cool my tongue; for I am in anguish in this flame* (Luke 16:24). What is this a picture of? This indicates there is another thing you will carry into the next world with you: you will carry the desires that you build up here. Hell is the place where desire and passion exist in their highest potency and where there is nothing to gratify them. You who are living in sin and worldliness, what are you doing? You are developing your soul passions and desires, until they become so predominant that you will find no gratification in the next world. Happy is that man or woman who sets their affection on the things above during this present life, rather than cultivating desires and aspirations for which there is no satisfaction in the next world. Wretched indeed is that man or woman who cultivates ruling powers, passions, and desires for which there is no gratification in the next world.

Shame

Hell is a place of shame, the awful heart-breaking agony of shame. In New York, we had a bank cashier who was in a hurry to get rich, so he appropriated the funds of the bank and invested them, intending to pay them back. But his investment was a failure. For a long time he kept the books in order to blind the bank examiner, but one day when the bank examiner was going over the books, he detected the embezzlement. He called in the cashier who had to acknowledge his fraud. He was arrested, tried, and sent to the state prison.

> Happy is that man or woman who sets their affection on the things above during this present life.

This banker had a beautiful wife and lovely child, a sweet, angel-like little girl. Sometime after his arrest and imprisonment, the little child came home sobbing with a breaking heart. "Oh," she said, "Mother, I can never go back to that school again. Send for my books."

Thinking it was some childish whim, the mother replied, "Oh, my darling, of course you will go back."

"No," she said, "Mother, I can never go back. Send for my books."

The mother said, "Darling, what is the matter?"

She said, "Another little girl said to me today, 'Your father is a thief.'"

Oh, the cruel stab! The mother saw that she could not go back to school. The wound was fatal. That fair blossom began to fade. A physician was called in, but the despair surpassed all the capacities of his art. The child faded and faded, until they laid her upon her bed, and the physician said, "Madam, I must tell you this is a case in which I am powerless; the child's heart has given way with the agony of the wound. Your child will die."

The mother went in and said to her dying child, "Darling, is there anything you would like to have me do for you?"

"Oh," she said, "yes, Mother; send for Father. Let him come home and lay his head on the pillow beside mine as he used to do."

Ah! but that was just what could not be done. The father was behind iron bars. They sent to the governor of the state, and he said, "I have no power in the matter."

They sent to the warden of the prison. He said, "I have no power in the matter."

But hearts were so touched that they got the judge and every member of the jury and the governor, and they formed a petition; they made arrangements whereby the father was allowed to come home under a deputy warden. He reached his home late at night and entered his house. The physician was waiting. He said, "I think you had better go in tonight, for I am afraid your child will not live until morning."

The father went to the door and opened it. The child looked quickly up. "Oh," she said, "I knew it was you, Father. I knew you would come. Father, come and lay your head beside mine on the pillow just as you used to do." And the strong man went and laid his head on the pillow; the child lovingly patted his cheek and died. Killed by shame. Hell is the place of shame, where everybody is dishonored.

Depraved Companionship

Hell is a place of vile companionships. Do you want to know the society of hell? Read Revelation 21:8: *The fearful, and unbelieving, and abominable, and murderers, and fornicators, and sorcerers, and idolaters, and all liars, their part shall be in the lake that burneth with fire and brimstone; which is the second death.*

That is the society of hell. "Oh," but somebody says, "many who are brilliant and gifted are going there." That may be true, but listen. How long will it take the most gifted man or woman to sink in such a world as that? Come to Chicago. I can go to the lowest disreputable establishments and pick out men who were once physicians, lawyers, congressmen, college professors, leading businessmen, and even ministers of the gospel but are now living with thugs, whoremongers, and everything that is vile and bad. How did they get there? They began to sink.

In 1864 when George B. McClellan was nominated on the democratic ticket for president of the United States, my father was one of the delegates to the presidential convention in Chicago. We then lived in New York. He took us with him nearly to the convention, left us in a quiet country town in Michigan, went on to the convention, and then came back for us; then we started back east. The train was filled with leading politicians. When we got to Albany, we left the train and got on a Hudson River steamboat. This steamboat was filled with the leading democratic politicians, and we had a political meeting for hours that evening. Man after man of our most gifted orators stood up and spoke to the crowd, but there was one man who stood there who eclipsed everyone else. As that man stood, everybody was spellbound by the power of his eloquence;

everybody was electrified, and as a boy of eight years of age, I was carried away with the marvelous eloquence of this man.

Years passed. One day I went out on our front lawn and saw something lying there, all covered with vomit, sleeping heavily, snoring like an overfed hog. When I went up to it, I found it was a man, and alas, it was the very man who that night had carried everyone on that ship by storm. He had wasted away. He died in a madhouse from alcohol and tobacco.

During our World's Fair, there was a women's board appointed to receive the dignitaries of the Old World, to receive the members of our nobility and the members of the royalty of Spain and other countries. A woman stood near Mrs. Potter Palmer, who was the ruling one of the Women's Commission, dazzling people by her beauty and by her wit. Just before I left Chicago to go around the world, some friends of mine went down to the slums of Chicago and hunted for poor forlorn people that they might help. They found a poor creature with nails grown like a bird's claws, long and tangled hair twisted full of filth, a face that had not been washed for weeks, and clad in a single filthy garment – a wreck! And when they talked with her, they discovered she was that woman who had stood so near Mrs. Potter Palmer during all the honors of the World's Fair. She had fallen through the use of cocaine.

Hopelessness

Hell is a world without hope. There are men who tell you that the word *aionios,* translated "everlasting," never means "everlasting"; but when they tell you that, they most likely have not looked into the matter, or they tell you a deliberate falsehood. It is true that it does not necessarily mean "everlasting." Whether it does or not has to be determined by the context. In Matthew 25:46, we read: *These shall go away into eternal punishment: but the righteous into eternal life,* and if it means "eternal" (everlasting) in one part of the verse, by every known law of exegesis it must mean the same in the other part of the verse. Nobody questions that it does mean "everlasting" in the one case.

Furthermore, there is another expression, *eis tous aionas ton aionon* (unto the ages of the ages), used twelve times in one book – eight times about the existence of God and the duration of His reign, once about the duration of the blessedness of the righteous, and in every remaining instance about the punishment, the beast, the false prophet, and the unrepentant. This declaration is the strongest known expression for absolute endlessness. Men, I have hunted through my Bible for one ray of hope for men who die unrepentant. I look for just a ray of hope for when the passage is properly interpreted by the right laws of exegesis, but I have failed after years of search to find one. I am familiar with the passages that men quote, but they will not bear the burden placed upon them when carefully interpreted in their context with an honest attempt to discover what they really mean without making them fit a theory. The New Testament does not hold out one ray of hope for those who die without Christ. Anyone who does, dares to do what God has not done. "Forever and ever" is the never-ceasing wail of that restless sea of fire. Such is hell, a place of bodily anguish, a place of agony of conscience, a place of insatiable torment and desire, a place of evil companionship, a place of shame, and a place without hope.

The New Testament does not hold out one ray of hope for those who die without Christ.

How Shall We Escape It?
That may be answered in a word. There is but one way to escape hell, and that is by the acceptance of Jesus Christ as your personal Savior – surrender to Him as your Lord and Master, confess Him before the world, and live a life of obedience,

demonstrating your faith. The Bible is perfectly plain about that. Acts 4:12 says, *There is none other name under heaven given among men, whereby we must be saved.* John 3:36 tells us that *he that believeth on the Son hath everlasting life: and he that believeth not the Son shall not see life; but the wrath of God abideth on him.*

In Matthew we read that *whosoever therefore shall confess me before men, him will I confess also before my Father which is in heaven. But whosoever shall deny me before men, him will I also deny before my Father which is in heaven* (Matthew 10:32-33). Second Thessalonians 1:7-9 says, *The Lord Jesus shall be revealed from heaven with his mighty angels, in flaming fire taking vengeance on them that know not God, and that obey not the gospel of our Lord Jesus Christ: who shall be punished with everlasting destruction from the presence of the Lord, and from the glory of his power.*

So the whole question is this: Will you accept Christ right now? Hell is too awful to risk it for a year; it is too awful to risk it for a month; it is too awful to risk it for a week; it is too awful to risk it for a day. Your eternal destiny and mine may be settled in twenty-four hours. It is too awful to risk it for an hour or even until I have finished my sermon. Take Christ now. I know what some of you are saying, or what the devil is whispering to you. He is saying, "Don't be a coward; don't be frightened into repentance."

Is it cowardice to be moved by rational fear? Is it heroism to rush into unnecessary danger? Suppose when I go out, I look up, and there is a building on fire. A man is sitting at an upper window reading a book. I see his peril, and I lift my hand to my mouth and say, "Flee for your life, the house is on fire!"

Then suppose that man should lean out of the window and shout back, "I am no coward. You can't frighten me." Would he be playing the hero, or would he be playing the fool?

One night I went to see my parents at the old home. They are both in heaven now. As I stepped off the one train, I stepped onto another track. Unknown to me, an express train was coming down that other track. A cabdriver of the town saw my peril, put his hand to his mouth, and cried, "Mr. Torrey, there is a train coming, get off the track!"

I did not shout back, "I am no coward; you can't scare me." I was not such a fool. No, I got off the track, or I would not be able to tell the story. You are on the track; I hear the not-far-distant thunder and rumble of the wrath of God as it comes hurrying on, and I cry, "Get off the track!" Receive Christ now! Take Him now! If you are reasonable, you will. If you don't, you will not be playing the hero, but playing the fool.

Chapter 4

God's Blockade to the Road to Hell

The Lord is not slack concerning his promise, as some men count slackness; but is longsuffering to us-ward, not willing that any should perish, but that all should come to repentance. (2 Peter 3:9)

If any man or woman in this audience is lost, it is not God's fault. God does not wish for you to be lost. God longs to have you saved. If God had His way, every man and woman would not only be saved sometime but would also be saved immediately. God is doing everything in His power to bring you to repentance. Of course, He cannot save you if you will not repent. You can have salvation if you want to be saved from sin, but sin and salvation can never go together.

Some people talk about a salvation in which man can continue in sin and still be saved. It is impossible. Sin is damnation, and if a man will go on forever in sin, he will be forever lost. But God is doing everything in His power to turn you out of the path of sin and destruction and into the path of righteousness and everlasting life. God has filled the path of sin – the path that leads to hell – with obstacles. He has made it hard and bitter. A great many people are saying today, "The Christian life is so hard." It is not. *[Christ's] yoke is easy, and [his] burden is light* (Matthew 11:30). God tells us in His Word that *the way of transgressors is hard* (Proverbs 13:15). God has filled it with obstacles, and you cannot continue in it without surmounting one obstacle after another. In this chapter, I will address some of the obstacles that God has put in the path of sin and ruin.

God's Obstacles

The Bible

The first one is the Bible. You cannot get very far in the path of sin without finding the Bible in your way. The Bible is one of the greatest hindrances to sin in the world. With its warnings, invitations, descriptions of the character and consequences of sin, representations of righteousness, its beauty and reward, and its pictures of God and His love, the Bible always stands as a great hindrance to sin. It makes men uneasy in sin. That is the reason many men hate the Bible; they are determined to sin, and the Bible makes them uneasy in sin, so they hate the Book.

The Bible is one of the greatest hindrances to sin in the world.

Men will give you many reasons why they object to the Bible, but in ninety-nine cases out of a hundred, if you trace men's objections, you will find the reason they hate the Bible is that it makes them uneasy in their sin. Men sometimes say to me, "I object to the Bible because of its filthy stories," but when I look at their lives, I find that their lives are filthy. The real objection is not to filthy stories, of which there are none. Stories of sin there are: stories that paint sin in its true colors, stories that make sin hideous. Their objection is not to filthy stories, but the Bible makes them uneasy in their filthy lives. This is why they hate it. The Bible makes it hard to continue in sin.

How often a man has been turned back from the path of sin by a single verse in the Bible. Hundreds of men have been turned out of the path of sin by Romans 6:23: *The wages of sin is death; but the free gift of God is eternal life in Christ Jesus our Lord.* Thousands of men have been turned out of the path of sin by Amos 4:12: *Prepare to meet thy God.* Tens of thousands of men have been turned out of the path of sin by John 3:16: *For God so loved the world, that he gave his only begotten Son, that whosoever believeth on him should not perish, but have eternal life;* and by John 6:37: *Him that cometh to me I will in no wise cast out.*

Several years ago a man came into our church in Chicago. He was a rampant infidel who had not been in a house of worship for fifteen or sixteen years. I don't know why he came in that night. I suppose he saw the crowd coming and was curious to know what was going on. He sat down, and I began to preach. In my sermon, I quoted John 6:37: *Him that cometh to me I will in no wise cast out.* It went like an arrow into that man's heart. When the meeting was over, he got up and went out and tried to forget that verse but could not. He went to bed but could not sleep. *Him that cometh to me I will in no wise cast out* kept ringing in his mind.

The next day it haunted him at work, and the next and the next, and for days and weeks that verse haunted him, but he was determined not to come to Christ. He came back to the street where our church stands, walked up and down the sidewalk, stomped his foot, and cursed the text, but he could not get rid of it. Six weeks passed, and he came into our prayer meeting, stood up, and said, "I was here six weeks ago and heard your minister preach. I heard the text John 6:37, and I have tried to forget it, but it has haunted me night and day. I have walked up and down the sidewalk in front of your church. I have stomped on the sidewalk and cursed the text, but I can't get rid of it. Pray for me." We did, and he was saved. One text from God's Word turned him out of the path of sin and ruin.

A Mother's Influence

The second obstacle that God has put in the path of sin is a mother's holy influence and teaching. Many hundreds of men and women are sitting in church services but are not yet Christians; they have tried to be infidels, tried to plunge into sin, but their mother's holy influence and Christian teaching won't let them go the way they desire. Sometimes it is years later that a mother's teaching does its work.

We had a young fellow who went west to Colorado in the mining times. He worked in the mines during the day and gambled at night, as so many miners do, but he spent more money gambling than he made in the mines. One night he was at the gaming table and lost his last cent. Then he used some of his employer's money and lost that. He felt he was ruined. He left the gaming table, went up into the mountains, drew his revolver, and held it to his temple. He was about to pull the trigger when a word that his mother had spoken to him years before came to his mind: "My son, if you are ever in trouble, think of God."

And there, standing in the moonlight with a revolver pressed against his temple and his finger on the trigger of the cocked revolver, he remembered what his mother had said. He dropped to his knees and cried to God. He was saved, turned out of the path to hell by a mother's teaching.

A Mother's Prayers

Another obstacle that God has put in the path of sin and ruin is a mother's prayers. In the desperate hardness of our hearts, we often trample our mother's teaching underfoot, but we find it very hard to get over her prayers. How often at the last moment a man is saved by his mother's prayers. In my church in Chicago, a man stood outside in the old days with a pitcher of beer as the people came out of the meeting and offered them a drink out of that pitcher of beer. He was hard and desperate and wicked, but he had a praying mother in Scotland. One night when he went home from the meeting where he had caused trouble, he was awakened in the middle of the night and was saved without getting out of bed, in answer to the prayers of a godly mother in Scotland.

This man went back to Scotland to see his mother. He also had a brother who was a sailor in the China seas; the mother and the saved son knelt down and prayed for the wandering boy, and that very night while they prayed, the Spirit of God came down upon that sailor, and he was saved. That brother, Dr. Morrison, became a missionary to India – saved by a mother's prayers.

I stand here, a saved man, because when I was rushing head-long into the path of sin and ruin, my mother's prayers rose, and I could not get over them. I used to think that nobody had anything to do with my salvation, no living being, for I was awakened in the middle of the night. I had gone to bed with no more thought of becoming a Christian than I had of jump-ing over the moon. In the middle of the night, I jumped out of bed and started to end my miserable life, but something came upon me, and I dropped to my knees; in five minutes from the time I got out of bed to take my life, I had surrendered to God. I thought no man or woman had anything to do with it, but I found out a woman had – my mother – 427 miles away praying, and while I had gotten over sermons and arguments and churches, I could not get over my mother's prayers. Do you know why some of you are not in hell right now? Your mother's prayers have kept you out of hell.

Sermons

Another obstacle is the sermons we hear. How many thousands and tens of thousands of men are turned back from sin to God by sermons that they hear or read. Sometimes the sermon does its work years after it is heard.

I remember one time in my first pastorate, I prepared a sermon on the parable of the ten virgins. One member of my congregation was very much on my heart; I prayed that the woman would be saved by that sermon. I preached that sermon and fully expected to see her saved, but when I gave the invitation, she never made a sign. I went home and did not know what to make of it. I said, "I prayed for her conversion by that sermon and fully expected her conversion, but she is not converted. I don't know what to make of it."

Years later when I had gone to another pastorate, I heard that this woman was converted. I revisited the place and called on her. I said, "I am very glad to hear you have been converted."

She said, "Would you like to know how I was converted?" I said I would. "Do you remember preaching a sermon years ago on the ten virgins? When you preached that sermon, I could not get it out of my mind. I felt I must take Christ that night, but I would not, and that sermon followed me, and I was converted years later by that sermon." I had been sure she would be converted by that sermon, but I did not see it for years.

Sunday School Teacher's Influence

Another obstacle is a Sunday school teacher's influence and teaching. They bring many to Christ. How many today have been brought to Christ by the teaching of a faithful Christian man or woman in the Sunday school? I want to say to you

Sunday school teachers that a faithful teacher is one of God's best instruments on earth for the salvation of the perishing.

In Mr. Moody's first Sunday school in Chicago, he had a class of very unruly girls; nobody could manage them, but finally he found a young man who was able to. One day this young man came into Mr. Moody's shop (it was before Mr. Moody went out of business) and said, "Mr. Moody," and he burst into tears.

Mr. Moody said, "What is the matter?"

"The doctor says I have tuberculosis and that I must go to California at once or die," and he sobbed as if his heart would break.

Mr. Moody tried to comfort him and said, "Suppose that is so; you have no occasion to feel so bad. You are a Christian."

"It is not that, Mr. Moody. I am perfectly willing to die, I am not afraid to die; but here I have had this Sunday school class all these years and not one of them in it is saved. I am going off to leave them, and everyone is unsaved," and he sobbed like a child.

Mr. Moody said, "Wait, I will get a carriage, and we will drive around and visit them; one by one you can lead them to Christ."

He took the pale teacher in the carriage, and they drove around to the homes of the girls; he talked to them about Christ until he was so tired that he had to be taken home. The next day they went out again, and they went out every day until every one of these women but one was saved. Then they all met for a prayer meeting before he went away. One after another led in prayer, and at last the one unsaved woman in the whole company led in prayer too and accepted Christ. He left by the early train the next morning, and Mr. Moody went down to the train to see him off. As they were waiting, one by one the women dropped in without any prearrangement, until every one of the young women was on the platform. He spoke a few words of farewell to them, and as the train pulled out of the station, he stood on the back platform of the car with his finger pointing heavenward, telling his Sunday school class to meet him in heaven.

Kindness

God often throws a kind word or act as an obstacle in the path of sin. A lady friend of mine was standing in a window looking out on Bleecker Street, New York. A drunkard came down the street. He had been a man in higher circumstances; he had been the mayor of a southern city but had declined from drink and was now a penniless drunkard on the streets of New York. He made up his mind to commit suicide and started for the river, but as he was going down Bleecker Street, he thought, "I will go into a tavern and have one more drink. I have spent a lot of money in that tavern, and I can certainly persuade the man for one drink."

He went in and asked for a drink; he told the man he had no money to pay for it, and the man came around from behind the bar and kicked him into the gutter. "You are welcome, man, as long as you have money," he said. My friend, looking out of the window, saw the poor wretch picking himself up out of the gutter. She crossed over and wiped the mud off with her handkerchief and said, "Come over here. It is bright and warm, and you will be welcome." So the poor wretch went over and sat down behind the stove. The meeting began, and one after another gave their testimony.

When it was over, that lady came and spoke to him about his soul; his heart was touched, and he was saved. He obtained a position and then earned a better one; finally he was made manager of one of the largest publishing houses in the city of

New York. One day he came to my friend and said, "I have some friends down at a hotel; I want you to meet them."

She went to the hotel, and he introduced her to a fine-looking middle-aged woman and a fine-looking young lady and said, "This is my wife and daughter." They were beautiful, refined, cultured ladies whom he had left when he descended to the very verge of hell, but the kind act and a word of invitation to Christ had turned him from the path to hell to the path that leads to glory. Let us go as the missionaries of God's grace to block the path of sinful people with kind deeds and thus turn them to righteousness and to God.

The Work of the Holy Spirit

Another obstacle that God puts in the path of sin and ruin is the Holy Spirit and His work. How strange it is. You and I have experienced it. When we were right in the midst of festivity, a strange feeling came into our hearts, an unrest, a dissatisfaction with the life we were living, a longing for something better, memories of home, church, mother, Bible, and God.

One night a man was playing cards at the table. He was wholly given up to the world; he belonged to a family of nobility, not a nobleman himself but connected with members of the nobility. But he was a wild, reckless, English spendthrift, and there he sat playing cards, when suddenly the voice of God's Spirit spoke in his heart. He thought he was about to die. He sprang up from the table, threw down his cards, and rushed to his room. There was someone in the room, and at first he thought, "It won't do to pray while the maid is in the room." But he was so convicted that he did not care; he dropped down by his bed and called upon God for Christ's sake to forgive his sins.

That man was Brownlow North, who did such a great work for God in Ireland and Scotland in 1859 and 1860. Listen, if you were in some den of infamy last night, was there a wretchedness, a sense of self-disgust, a longing for something better, a calling to a purer life that came into your heart? What was it? God's Spirit. As you consider this today, there is a stirring in your heart, and you are saying to yourself, "I wonder if I had better not become a Christian tonight." You may have almost a determination to stand up as soon as the invitation is given. What is it? God sending His Spirit to blockade the road to hell. Listen to God's Spirit right now. Yield to Him and accept Christ.

The Cross of Christ

The cross of Christ is one other obstacle that God has put in the road as a blockade in the path to hell. No man can get very far down the path of sin and ruin before he sees the cross looming in front of him. On that cross there hangs

If you continue in sin, you will have to pass by the cross and the crucified form of the Son of God.

a man, the Son of Man, the Son of God. You see Him hanging there with nails in His hands and feet, and a voice says, "It was for you. I bore this for you; I died for you." In the pathway of every man and woman today stands the cross with Christ on it; if you go out and continue in sin, you will have to pass by the cross and the crucified form of the Son of God.

I heard of a godly old man who had a worthless son. That son was more anxious to make money than he was for honor or anything else, and he determined to go into that infamous business in which there is lots of money, but which no self-respecting man will undertake – the liquor business. Any man who is willing to earn money by selling alcohol will earn money out of the tears of brokenhearted wives, the groans and sighs of the drunkards' sons and daughters, and the hearts' blood of their fellow man because this infernal alcohol traffic is sending thousands of men to premature graves every year. This infernal alcohol traffic is causing more sorrow, more ruined homes, and more wretchedness than perhaps anything else on earth, and every pub owner, every barman, every barmaid, and every professed Christian who owns stock in breweries or distilleries is a party to the crime. You have plenty to say about the alcohol seller and the bartender. I would like to know how he is any worse than professing Christians who own brewery stock. He gets the abuse, and you get the money, but you will get the eternal damnation unless you get out of the infernal business.

Well, this man had lost his self-respect to such an extent that he was going to open a tavern; his father was ashamed. He pleaded with him. He said, "My boy, you bear an honored name which has never been disgraced before. Don't disgrace it by putting it up over a tavern." But the son was so intent on making money that he would not listen to his father's voice. The day came to open the tavern. The father was about the first to arrive. He stood outside the door of that bar and stepped up to every man that approached the door. He told them of the miseries that came from strong drink and warned them of the consequences of entering such a place. One after another, they turned away.

The son looked out the window to see why he was getting no customers. He saw his father outside, turning his customers away. He came outside and said, "Father, go home. You are ruining my business."

The father answered, "I cannot help it, my boy. I won't have my name dishonored by this business, and if you are determined to go on with it, I will stand here and warn every man that comes to enter your door."

Finally the son lost his temper and struck his old father. I tell you, this alcohol business takes the humanity out of people; he struck his old father in the face. The father turned to him without the least bit of anger. He said, "My son, you can strike me if you will; you can kill me if you will, but no man shall enter your tavern unless he goes over my dead body."

No man or woman will ever enter hell unless they trod over the dead body of Jesus Christ. No man or woman can go out, refusing Christ and persisting in sin, without trampling underfoot the form of Jesus who was crucified on the cross of Calvary for you.

God has piled the obstacles so high in His patient love! Don't try to conquer them. Turn back. Turn out of the path of sin; turn into the path of faith in Jesus Christ. Turn now!

Chapter 5

Heaven: What It Is, and How to Get There

He looked for the city which hath the foundations, whose builder and maker is God. (Hebrews 11:10)

We have not here an abiding city, but we seek after the city which is to come. (Hebrews 13:14)

I go to prepare a place for you. (John 14:2)

And he shall wipe away every tear from their eyes; and death shall be no more; neither shall there be mourning, nor crying, nor pain, any more: the first things are passed away. (Revelation 21:4)

My subject in this chapter is heaven: what it is, and how to get there. This was the city Abraham sought, *the city which hath the foundations;* this is the *abiding city* which we are seeking instead of these fleeting and perishable cities and homes of earth. What sort of a place is this city? What sort of a place is heaven? In answer to the question, I won't tell what sort of a place I imagine heaven to be. I care very little for my speculations or any other man's speculations and notions on this point. I will tell you something that is sure. I will tell you what God plainly teaches about it in His Word.

Many think we know nothing about heaven, and that it is all guesswork. That is not so. God has revealed much about it, and what He has revealed about it is very heartening and eminently calculated to awaken in every wise and true heart a desire to go there. I think if we reflected more about heaven, it would help us to bear our burdens here more bravely; it would encourage us to holier living and help deliver us from the power of the greed and the lust that is impairing so many lives. Focusing more on heaven would make us cheerier and more pleasant.

Focusing more on heaven would make us cheerier and more pleasant.

Philosophers who tell us that our present business is to live this present life and let the future take care of itself are very shallow. You might as well tell the schoolboy that his present business is to live today and take no care about the future life of manhood and not wisely prepare for it and feel its stimulus. True thoughts of the life that is to come clothe the present life with new beauty and strength. Let us then think a while about heaven. What do we know about it?

Heaven, a Place

First, heaven is a place. *I go to prepare a place for you,* says Jesus (John 14:2). Some will tell you that heaven is merely a state or condition. Doubtless, it is more important to be in a heavenly state or condition than in a heavenly place. It would unquestionably be preferable to be in hell in a heavenly state of thought and heart than to be in heaven in a hellish state of thought and heart. But heaven is a place. We are not to merely be in a heavenly state of mind but in a heavenly city as well, a *city which hath the foundations, an abiding city.* Christ has already entered into heaven now to appear in the presence of God for us (Hebrews 9:24). He has gone to prepare a place for us and is coming back for us to take us to it. We are not to be disembodied spirits in the world to come, but redeemed spirits, in redeemed bodies, in a redeemed society, in a redeemed universe.

Characteristics of Heaven

Heaven is first a place of incomparable external as well as internal beauty. This appears from such descriptions as we have in Revelation 21 and 22. The God of the Bible is a God of beauty. The God of nature is also a God of beauty. He made this world beautiful, but its beauty has been marred by sin; the weed and the thorn and the brier spring up; the insect devours the roses; the lilies fade; and decay and death bring loathsome sights and foul smells. *The whole creation,* fallen in sympathy with fallen man, *groaneth and travaileth in pain together until now* (Romans 8:22). But enough is left of the original beauty to show us how intensely God loves beauty, and He has told us in His Word that *the creation itself also shall be delivered from the bondage of corruption into the liberty of the glory of the children of God* (Romans 8:21).

In heaven there will be the perfection of beauty – perfection of form, color, sound, and odor. The beauty that is to be is indescribable. All earthly comparisons fail. Every sense and faculty of perception in our present state is blunted by sin and the disease that results from sin. But in our redemptive bodies, every sense and faculty will receive enlargement and exist in perfection. We cannot imagine what new senses we might have. Every faculty will have unlimited opportunity for exercise. A material beauty, the counterpart of the moral beauty of that world, the highest and most faultless, will surround us on every side, filling eye and ear and nostrils.

Some of us have seen beautiful visions on earth. We have seen the mountains rearing their snow-crowned heads through the clouds; we have seen the vistas of rolling hills and lush valleys with winding rivers and forests and their changing colors. We have seen the lake and ocean dancing, tossing, and rolling in the moonlight; we have seen the heavens in the clear wintry night bejeweled with their countless stars; and we have caught the odors that float through the summer night in parks and gardens and tropical islands. We have listened to the indescribable harmonies of piano and violin and organ as they responded to the touch of the master's hand and the more matchless music of the human voice, but all these are nothing compared to the beauty of sight and sound and fragrance that will greet us in that fair city that has foundations. This shall be the reward of the poorest of God's children. That poor widow, who toils by the dim candlelight for a pitifully small wage with which unadorned sweaters reward her painful toil, will soon be at rest and enter upon these scenes of indescribable beauty forever.

Companionships in Heaven

But the beauty of heaven, as good and attractive as it is, will be its least important characteristic. Heaven will be a place of high, holy, and ennobling companionships. The best and wisest and noblest men of all ages will be there. Abraham and Isaac and Jacob will be there.

Matthew 8:11 says, *And I say unto you, that many shall come from the east and the west, and shall sit down with Abraham, and Isaac, and Jacob, in the kingdom of heaven,* along with

Moses, Elijah, and Daniel, Paul and John, Rutherford and Brainerd and Payson.

All the purest, noblest, most unselfish ones the world has known will be there. All those who have trusted in the atoning blood of Christ – *For we know that if the earthly house of our tabernacle be dissolved, we have a building from God, a house not made with hands, eternal, in the heavens* (2 Corinthians 5:1). All the dear ones who believed in and loved the Lord Jesus will be there.

There are many who desire to get into the best society of earth, and that is all right, if really it is the best society and not merely the society of wealth, fashion, and foolishness that is sometimes strangely and irrationally called "the best society." But the very best society of this world will be nothing compared to the society of heaven. The joys we find in the dearest companionships of noble, unselfish, thoughtful people here give but the faintest concept of the joys of heaven's companionships.

> The joys we find in the dearest companionships people here give but the faintest concept of the joys of heaven's companionships.

The angels are in heaven. Luke 1:19 says, *And the angel answering said unto him, I am Gabriel, that stand in the presence of God; and I was sent to speak unto thee, and to bring thee these good tidings.* Later in Luke we read: *I say unto you, that even so there shall be joy in heaven over one sinner that repenteth, more than over ninety and nine righteous persons, who need no repentance. Even so, I say unto you, there is joy in the presence of the angels of God over one sinner that repenteth* (Luke 15:7, 10).

We shall enjoy the companionship of these lofty intelligences – Gabriel, Raphael, with the whole angelic host.

God Himself is there too. In a sense He is everywhere, but heaven is the place of His particular presence and the manifestation of Himself. Several Scriptures illustrate this: *Then hear thou from heaven thy dwelling-place* (2 Chronicles 6:30). *Thy kingdom come. Thy will be done, as in heaven, so on earth* (Matthew 6:10). We shall hold communion with Him. Jesus Christ is there: *And said, Behold, I see the heavens opened, and the Son of man standing on the right hand of God* (Acts 7:56). *Seeing then that we have a great high priest, that is passed into the heavens, Jesus the Son of God, let us hold fast our profession* (Hebrews 4:14). *Now in the things which we are saying the chief point is this: We have such a high priest, who sat down on the right hand of the throne of the Majesty in the heavens* (Hebrews 8:1).

To Paul this was one of the most attractive thoughts about heaven: *But I am in a strait betwixt the two, having the desire to depart and be with Christ; for it is very far better* (Philippians 1:23). Samuel Rutherford also cried, "I would rather be in hell with Thee than in heaven without Thee; for, if I were in hell with Thee, that would be heaven to me, and if I were in heaven without Thee, that would be hell to me."

On the other hand, there will be no unpleasant or degrading companionships there. The devil will not be there. The lewd, the vulgar, and the obscene will not be there. The greedy, the scheming, and the selfish will not be there. The liar, the slanderer, the backbiter, the meddler, and the gossiper will not be there. The mean, the contemptible, and the hypocrite will not be there. The profane, the blasphemer, the infidel, and the scoffer will not be there. No money, influence, or cunning will get them in. *And there shall in no wise enter into it anything unclean, or he that maketh an abomination and a lie* (Revelation 21:27).

Heaven will be a good place to be. Your city would not be such a bad place to live if we could get rid of some of its inhabitants. All such will be gotten rid of in heaven. There are limitations to the joys of the dearest earthly companionships. Here –

Thought is deeper than all speech,
Feeling deeper than all thought;
Souls to souls can never teach
What unto themselves was taught.[2]

It will not be like that there. We will perfectly open our hearts to one another, as we so often long to here. *For now we see in a mirror, darkly; but then face to face: now I know in part; but then shall I know fully even as also I was fully known* (1 Corinthians 13:12).

Heaven will be a place of glad reunions. Then we who are alive, who remain, will be caught up together with them in the clouds to meet the Lord in the air, and so we will always be with the Lord (1 Thessalonians 4:17). The bereaved wife shall meet the husband she has missed for so long; the son shall meet the mother whose departure left his life so desolate. There we shall meet again children who were removed from us in all the beauty of their early life and whom we have never forgotten through all the months and years that have passed. Ah, what glad days those coming days will be when we meet again – nevermore to part.

Freedom from Sin

Heaven will be a place that is free from everything that curses or mars our life here. The world we live in would be a happy place indeed, if it were not for a few things. If there were no sin, no sickness, no pain, no poverty, no labor, no lack, and no death, this world would be good. But these things mar and almost ruin this present world. There will be none of these things in heaven. There will be no sin. Everyone will perfectly obey the will of God. There will be no poverty. Everyone will

---

2   Christopher Pearse Cranch, "Thought," 1844.

have all the inexhaustible wealth of God at his disposal. *And if children, then heirs; heirs of God, and joint-heirs with Christ; if so be that we suffer with him, that we may be also glorified together* (Romans 8:17).

There will be no menial, grinding toil. When I see the weary women who toil from early morning until late at night over a washtub or ironing board or sewing machine, when I see the men who rise at the break of day and go to the forge or bench or ditch, I rejoice that there is a place where the weary can rest. There will be none of these things in heaven. *There remaineth therefore a sabbath rest for the people of God* (Hebrews 4:9).

There will be no sickness nor pain. And God *shall wipe away every tear from their eyes; and death shall be no more; neither shall there be mourning, nor crying, nor pain, any more: the first things are passed away* (Revelation 21:4). No more aching limbs, no more throbbing temples, no more darting pains, no more grinding tortures, no more swelling tongues, no more weakness, no more sighs, no more groans, no more nights of tossing in sweltering rooms, no more tears.

There will be no death in heaven. No breaking hearts as we look for the last time into the faces of loved ones as cheeks grow ashen and eyes glaze over. No watching the undertaker as he fastens down the coffin lid on the one we loved; no black dresses and veils. There will be no funerals passing through the streets, no standing by a cavernous grave to watch a coffin lowered into it, and no listening to the cold lumps of soil as they fall remorselessly on the box that contains the form of the one we love so much and whose departure leaves life so cheerless. Thank God, there is no death in heaven.

Perfect Knowledge

Heaven will be a place of universal and perfect knowledge. Here the wisest of us sees through a glass darkly, but there face-to-face. Here we know in part, but there we will know even as we are known (1 Corinthians 13:12). The wisest scientist or philosopher on earth knows very little. The little they do know is exceedingly precious, but it is very little. When he was an old man, Sir Isaac Newton said to one who praised his wisdom, "I am as a child on the seashore picking up a pebble here and a shell there, but the great ocean of truth still lies before me." But in heaven the

Heaven will be a place of perfect knowledge. God's wondrous purposes and their accomplishment will lie open before us.

most uneducated of us will have fathomed that great ocean of truth – perfect knowledge of all things. The great perplexing problems of God and man, of time and eternity, will be solved. God's wondrous purposes and their accomplishment will lie open before us. No doubts, no questionings, no uncertainties, no errors. Faith swallowed up in sight.

Perfect Love

Heaven will be a place of universal and perfect love. *Beloved, now are we children of God, and it is not yet made manifest what we shall be. We know that, if he shall be manifested, we shall be like him; for we shall see him even as he is* (1 John 3:2). We shall be like Him, and He is love. *He that loveth not knoweth not God; for God is love* (1 John 4:8).

What a place to live: where everyone is a lover and where all love is perfect. How happy is the home where love is triumphant. It may be a lowly home, a very plain place, but it is a happy place. *Better is a dinner of herbs, where love is, than a stalled ox and hatred therewith* (Proverbs 15:17). All is love there. And that love will not be like that of earth – hesitating, suspicious, uncertain, selfish, first cold and then warm – but will be pure, unbounded, unfaltering, unchanging, constant, and Christlike. What a world that will be! The universal brotherhood of which we read and talk about and see so little of will find its perfect realization in heaven.

Place of Praise

Heaven will be a place of praise:

> *After these things I saw, and behold, a great multitude, which no man could number, out of every nation and of all tribes and peoples and tongues, standing before the throne and before the Lamb, arrayed in white robes, and palms in their hands; and they cry with a great voice, saying, Salvation unto our God who sitteth on the throne, and unto the Lamb. And all the angels were standing round about the throne, and about the elders and the four living creatures; and they fell before the throne on their faces, and worshipped God, saying, Amen: Blessing, and glory, and wisdom, and thanksgiving, and honor, and power, and might, be unto our God for ever and ever. Amen* (Revelation 7:9-12).

Men will have open eyes to see God as He is, to see Jesus Christ as He is. Souls will throb and burst forth with praise. Suppose we should get one glimpse of God as He is, one view of Jesus Christ as He is! There would be a burst of song rising from all of us such as never rang before. There will be melody all day long in heaven. Some people ask me in a critical way, Why do you have so much music in your meetings? Because we wish them to be as much like heaven as possible. Heaven will be a very musical place. There will be far more singing than preaching there.

An Abiding City with Foundations

Heaven will be a *city which hath the foundations, an abiding city* (Hebrews 11:10; 13:14). Earth's greatest cities and earth's fairest homes do not abide; they crumble into dust. The so-called eternal city of the past is trodden underneath the unheeding feet of the beggars of modern Rome. The world itself does not abide. *The world passeth away* (1 John 2:17). Heaven continues. We enter it and go out no more – ever. The eons of eternity roll on, but heaven abides in its beauty, in its glory, in its joyousness, and in its love; and we abide with it.

Gaining an Entrance into Heaven

Is no heart stirred with a longing for that *better country* (Hebrews 11:16)? Who would not rather have an entrance into heaven than to have the poor fleeting possessions of any of earth's millionaires? If I had to choose between having the most splendid mansion on earth with the largest fortune and all that **Christ is the way to God. Accept Christ; accept Him fully as your Savior.** money could buy, and miss heaven or live in the most wretched tenement in need and hunger and suffering all my days but gain heaven in the end, it would not take long to choose.

When we reach that fair home, the hardships of earth through which we may have passed will seem small and trifling indeed. *I reckon that the sufferings of this present time are not worthy to be compared with the glory which shall be revealed to us-ward* (Romans 8:18). But we may all gain an entrance. There is only one way, but that way is very simple and open to all. *Jesus saith unto him, I am the way, and the truth, and the life: no one cometh unto the Father, but by me* (John 14:6). And in John 10:9, He says, *I am the door; by me if any man enter in, he shall be saved, and shall go in and go out, and shall find pasture.*

Christ is the door to heaven; Christ is the way to God. Accept Christ; accept Him fully as your Savior, your Master, and your Lord. Do it today. Do it now. If you stood outside the door of some fair mansion where all inside was beauty, and sociability, and joyousness, and love, and the owner said, "Come in," would you wait for a second invitation and risk it not being given? But even now Jesus swings heaven's door open wide and says, "Come in." Accept Him at once and gain a right to enter and live forever in heaven.

In the United States, there was a godless father who had a sweet little child who was an earnest Christian. This young daughter fell ill and died. The father was very angry at God. After the funeral, he raged around his room, cursing God who had taken his beloved child from him. At last, utterly worn out, he threw himself upon the bed and fell asleep. In his sleep he dreamed that he stood beside a dark river and saw a beautiful land on the far side. As he gazed across the river, he saw children coming toward him. From among the children, one fair child emerged, whom he recognized as his own little daughter. She was beckoning to him and calling, "Come over here, Father, come over here." He awoke, burst into tears, and gave up his rebellion against God; he accepted Christ and prepared to meet his child in the fair land beyond the river.

To many of us there are voices of loved ones who have gone before, calling, "Come over here, Father"; "Come over here, my son"; "Come over here, Mother"; "Come over here, Husband"; "Come over here, Wife." Let us accept Christ at once and gain the right to enter heaven and live there forever.

Chapter 6

The New Birth

Ye must be born again. (John 3:7)

No one can be saved unless he is born again by the power of God's Holy Spirit. *Ye must be born again,* says Jesus. The necessity is absolute; not merely, "You *may* be born again," but "You *must* be born again."

Born Again

Nothing else will take the place of the new birth. Neither baptism nor confirmation will take the place of the new birth. Simon, in the eighth chapter of the Acts of the Apostles, was baptized, and whatever the right form of water baptism may be, he was baptized the right way, for he was baptized by a man sent by the apostles and taken into the early church. But when Peter and John came down and saw his heart, Peter said unto him, *Thou hast neither part nor lot in this matter: for thy heart is not right before God. For I perceive that thou art in the gall of bitterness, and in the bond of iniquity* (Acts 8:21, 23). A baptized lost sinner! I go to people and ask them to come to Christ, but they say, "I have been baptized; I have been confirmed." Have you been born again? *Ye must be born again.*

No performance of religious duties will take the place of the new birth. A great many people are depending on the fact that they say their prayers, read their Bibles, go to church, partake of Communion, and perform other duties, but all that will not take the place of the new birth. *Ye must be born again.*

Orthodoxy of faith will not take the place of the new birth. Many people say, "I believe the Apostles' Creed," "I believe the Nicene Creed," "I believe in the Larger Catechism and the Shorter Catechism," "I am orthodox; I hold the right views about Christ, the right views about the Bible, the right views about the atonement." You can be "orthodox" on every doctrine and be lost forever. I suppose the devil is as orthodox as a person can be. The devil knows the truth about the Bible. He hates it and loves to get others to believe something else, but he believes it himself. The devil knows the truth about Christ. He believes in the divinity of Christ. He tries to keep others from believing it, but he believes it himself; he knows Jesus Christ is divine. The devil believes the truth about hell. No one knows better than the devil that there is an everlasting hell. In that sense, the devil is perfectly orthodox, but yet he is damned. *Ye must be born again.*

> Culture, refinement, and outward correctness of life will not take the place of the new birth.

Culture, refinement, and outward correctness of life will not take the place of the new birth. The trouble with us is not merely in our outward life. The trouble is also in the heart. The corruption is in the heart, in the very deepest depths of our inner life, and merely to reform your outward life is not enough; that will not save you. It does not go deep enough.

Suppose I had a rotten apple. I could take that apple to an

artist and have him put a coating of wax around it and then paint it until it was just as beautiful in appearance as any apple you ever saw, but it would be just as rotten as ever. Take one bite into it, and you bite into the decay. The trouble with people is that outside of Christ they are rotten at the heart, and mere culture, mere refinement, mere respectability, mere reform, and mere morality is simply putting a coating of wax on the outside and painting it.

You must be changed down to the deepest depths of your being. What we need is the power of God going down to the deepest depths of our souls, banishing death, and bringing in life – banishing corruption and bringing in the holiness of God. *Follow . . . holiness, without which no man shall see the Lord* (Hebrews 12:14), and it is only by the regenerating power of the Spirit of God that any man or woman can become holy. *Ye must be born again.*

The necessity of the new birth is universal. No man or woman on the face of the earth will ever see the kingdom of God or enter the kingdom of God unless they are born again. There are no exceptions. No woman in your city, however refined, highly educated, amiable, or beautiful in her daily life will ever see the kingdom of God unless she is born again.

If anybody could have entered the kingdom of God without the new birth, it was Nicodemus. He was an upright man and honored by everyone; he moved in the best society as a man of wealth and culture. He belonged to the orthodox party, a man of deep religious earnestness, sincerely desiring to know the right way. Nicodemus was a man who prayed and studied his Bible and went to the synagogue several times a week. The Lord Jesus looked him right in the face and said, "Nicodemus, you must be born again. No exceptions. *Except a man be born again, he cannot see the kingdom of God* (John 3:3)."

So I come to you with the question, Have you been born

again? I do not ask if you are a church member. I do not ask if you believe the truth. I do not ask if you say your prayers or read your Bible. I do not ask if you go to church. I do not ask if you have a liberal heart towards the poor. I do not ask if you give to foreign missions. Have you been born again?

Transformation

"Well," somebody says, "what does it mean to be born again?" As good a definition as I know is given in 2 Corinthians 5:17: *Wherefore if any man is in Christ, he is a new creature* [creation]: *the old things are passed away; behold, they are become new.* The new birth is a new creation. A radical transformation by the power of the Spirit of God in the deepest depths of our being – a new will, new affections, and new thoughts. We are born with a perverted will. We are born with corrupted affections. We are born with a blinded mind.

In regeneration by the power of the Holy Spirit, God transforms our will, transforms our affections and our tastes, and transforms our way of looking at things. Every man and woman by nature has a perverted will, a will that is set on pleasing self. By nature we love to please ourselves. We do what pleases ourselves, and that may not be vicious at all; we may not be pleased to get drunk, or swear, or lie, or do anything vicious or vulgar, but yet our minds are bent on pleasing ourselves.

But when God imparts to us His nature, our will is changed and so is the whole purpose of our life.

But when God, by His Spirit, imparts to us His nature and life, our will is changed and so is the whole purpose of our life. The whole will is surrendered to God, and we live to please Him. We may do a great many things we did before, but now we do them because they please God.

Before, we did them because they pleased ourselves. Our affections are corrupt by nature. We loved the things we shouldn't love and hated the things we ought to love. For example, many women love novels, which God hates; they love them more than they love the Bible, which God loves. If many women were to stand up and speak the truth, they would say, "I would rather read a storybook any day of the week than read the Bible."

Many of you love the theater, which God hates. I don't say God hates theatrical people; He loves them, but He hates the theater. God hates the card table; I am sure He does. You all would too, probably, if you knew as much about it as I do, but you love the card table.

God hates dances. I would think that any intelligent, modest person would too, if they only stopped to think a little, but many of you love dances. You would rather go to the theater than to the gathering of God's children. If you had your choice Wednesday night or Thursday night between going to a first-class opera or to a place where God's Spirit was present in power, you would choose the opera. You would go to a card party rather than to a quiet gathering of God's people, where they kneel down and pray for the outpouring of the Spirit, and very likely you are a church member.

Love of the Bible

When God, through the power of the Spirit, imparts to you a new nature, you will love the Bible more than any other book in the world. You will love the place where God manifests Himself more than any place of worldly entertainment. You will love the company of God's people more than you will love the pleasures of this world. And the beautiful thing is that in a moment of time, by the power of God's Holy Spirit, the change comes.

New tastes and new affections take the place of the old tastes and old affections. There is no one who loves the theater more than I once did – and the dance. I used to attend four to six dances a week. Or anyone that loves a card party more than I once did, for I played cards every day of my life except on Sunday. (I thank God that my mother's training at least kept me from doing it on Sunday.) You could not hire me to do those things today. I think there is not enough money in this city to hire me to go to the theater, unless I went there to get some poor soul out. There is not enough money to get me to play whist, or casino, or bridge, or anything else. I hate it. I love the things I once hated, and I hate the things I once loved. Why, in those days I would rather have read any novel than have read this Book. Today I have more joy in reading this Book than in any other book on earth. I love it.

My greatest intellectual joy is just to pore over the wonderful pages of this Book of God. Then you will get new thoughts. Many of you today are blind to the divine authority of this Book. You believe all the nonsense that people tell you in the name of what they call "scholarship" about the mistakes in it. When you are born again, you will get a mind so in tune with the mind of God that you will believe everything in it in spite of what everybody says.

Some of you cannot believe the doctrine of the atonement, that Jesus took our sins in His own body on the cross. The preaching of this doctrine is foolishness to those who are perishing (1 Corinthians 1:18), but when you are born again, the doctrine that the Son of God died on the cross of Calvary will be one of the sweetest doctrines in all the universe. You will have a new will set upon pleasing God instead of pleasing self, new affections to love the things that God loves and hate the things that God hates, and a new mind about the truth of God. Have you been born again? If not, you are not saved. *Verily,*

verily, I say unto thee, Except one be born anew, he cannot see the kingdom of God (John 3:3).

Practicing Righteousness

How can we tell whether we have been born again or not? First John 2:29 says, *Every one also that doeth righteousness is begotten of him.* If you have been born of God, you will do as God does. God does righteousness. If you are born of God, righteousness will be the practice of your life. What is righteousness? It is doing that which is right in God's sight. A man who is born of God will study the Word of God to find out what God's will is as revealed in His Word, and when he finds it out, he will do it. Are you doing that? Studying the Word of God daily to discover what God wants you to do? When you find out what God wants you to do, are you doing it?

Whosoever is begotten of God doeth no sin (1 John 3:9). That is, that person does not make a practice of sin. John tells us what he means by *sin* a few verses before this. To commit sin is to do that which you know to be contrary to God's will. When he knows God's will, the man of God will not disobey it. He may be mistaken. He may do something that he did not realize at the time was not God's will. But he will discover it was not, and when he does, he will admit it and confess it as sin. Or he may be suddenly surprised, overtaken by a sudden temptation, and fall; but as soon as he recognizes it, he will confess it. He will not continue day after day doing that which he knows to be contrary to the will of God.

Anybody who is regularly making a practice of something that they know to be contrary to the will of God has reason to doubt whether they are born again. A young man asked me on the street on Thursday, "If a man is born again and lies down in sin and dies in sin, will he be saved?"

"Why," I said, "a man who is born again will not lie down in sin. He may fall into it, but he will not stay there."

Do you know the difference between a hog and a sheep? A hog will fall into the mud, and when he gets there, he will stay there. A sheep may fall into the mud, but he gets up as quickly as he can. Many people that we think are Christ's sheep are only washed hogs, or sows. A sow that is washed will return to the mire, but a sheep will not stay in the mud. Some of you say, "I wish Dr. Torrey would not use such inelegant language." It is not my language, it is God's. If you are only outwardly reformed, if you are simply externally converted, in a few weeks you will go back to your sin and your worldliness. You are only a washed sow. I am quoting Scripture. It is God's language (2 Peter 2:22). The person who is outwardly converted but not inwardly transformed will give up after a little while, but if you have been born again, you are transformed from a sow into a sheep, and you will never be down in sin again.

Love of the Brethren

You find the third proof of regeneration in 1 John 3:14 – love of the brethren. *We know that we have passed out of death into life, because we love the brethren* – love for everybody that belongs to Christ, irrespective of their social position and irrespective of their race or color. We love the brethren, every child of God. The nature of God is love, and if God has imparted His nature to you, you have a heart full of love, and especially love for God's children.

I once went to a Communion service in the city of Brooklyn, and they were receiving new members. A lady sat near me, and when the people stood up to receive the new members, I saw that she did not stand up. When the meeting ended, I said to her (I knew her very well), "Why didn't you stand up to receive the new members?"

She replied, "I was not going to stand up for them. They are our mission people. I am not going to love and watch over and care for them."

They were poor and she was rich. She was not a child of God. You will love the poorest old washerwoman who is born of God just as much as if she were the wife of a millionaire. A woman who cannot read or write you will love just as much as if she were the most highly educated woman in the kingdom. It is a practical love, a love that shows itself by going into the pocket.

People will get up in a prayer meeting sometimes and say, "I know I have passed from death unto life because I love the brethren."

After the meeting a lady goes around and says, "There is Mrs. Smith; she is in trouble. She needs a little help, and we are taking a collection for her. Won't you give something?"

And the first woman says, "I cannot do it. Christmas is coming, and I must get presents for my sisters, and children, and cousins, and I cannot give to everybody." You can, if you are a child of God and have it to give.

The Bible is such a practical book for everyday life. The proof of the new birth is love, and the proof of love is that if you have a penny left in your pocket, you will go and share it with your poor brethren, your poor sisters – if you are born again.

Jesus Is the Christ

Another test is in 1 John 5:1: *Whosoever believeth that Jesus is the Christ is begotten of God.* Now, you say, "I agree with that. I believe that Jesus is the Christ." Do you? "Of course I do. I am perfectly orthodox." It is not orthodoxy, it is real belief. *Christ* means "King," and if you really believe in Christ as King, it leads you to set Him up as King in your heart. Does Christ sit upon the throne of your heart? Does Christ rule your life? If He does, you are born of God. If He doesn't, you are not.

First John 5:4 says, *Whatsoever is begotten of God overcometh the world.* There are two classes of people in the world – those who are overcoming the world and those who are being overcome by the world. Which class do you belong to? Are you getting the victory over the world, or is the world getting the victory over you? Many people come to me and say, "I know this is not just right, but it is what everybody here does, and so I do it."

The world is getting the victory over you. "I don't believe in this, but all the people in our suburb, even including the church members, do it; therefore I do it." The world is getting the victory over you. If you are born of God, you will get the victory over the world. You won't ask what the world does; you will ask what Christ says, and you will obey Christ, your King. You will get the victory over the world, though you have to stand alone. Are you born of God? *Ye must be born again.* Have you been born again?

I think many of you will say, "No, I haven't. Can you tell me now what I must do to be born again?" Yes, I can. God Himself tells us.

John 1:12 says, *As many as received him, to them gave he the right to become the children of God.* We are born again by God's Holy Spirit, through His Word, the moment we receive Christ. When you take Christ into your heart, you take the life of God into your heart. When you take Christ into your heart, Christ comes and reigns and transforms you through and through in a moment. Anybody, however worldly, sinful, hard, or unbelieving they are, can become a new creature. Anyone today who will throw his heart open to let Jesus come in to rule and reign and take Him as his sin-bearing Savior, his deliverer from the power of sin, can be born again the moment you surrender the control of your life to Him. God, by the power of His Holy Spirit, will make you a new creature.

Some people will present two persons. One has been carefully reared and taught to observe the outward forms of Christianity, and the other has descended into the deepest depths of sin. They will say, "Here is this person very near the kingdom; she will surely be easily led to accept Christ. But here this other person has descended into the depths of sin; of course, we don't expect to see that one saved right now."

Why not? If that moral, refined, amiable, beautiful girl takes Christ, then God by His Holy Spirit will impart His nature to her and make her a child of God the moment she does it. But if the vilest woman in this city takes Christ, then God by His Holy Spirit will impart His nature to her and make her a child of God the moment she does it. How often I have seen this– even at the same meeting.

There is not a person within the hearing of my voice who cannot become a child of God right now.

Ye must be born again. You can be born again. There is not a person within the hearing of my voice who cannot become a child of God right now if he will take the Lord Jesus Christ. The moment he does, God, by a creative act, by the power of His Holy Spirit, will make him a new creature. *Old things are passed away; behold, all things are become new* (2 Corinthians 5:17).

Two thoughts I wish to leave with you. First, that the most highly educated, most upright, most amiable, most attractive man or woman who is without Christ will never be saved except by the creative act of God when the Holy Spirit in the inmost depths of their soul makes them a new creation in Christ.

Second, the most hopelessly abandoned man or woman in your city can be saved in an instant, born again, made a new creature, the moment they accept Christ. We are all saved the same way: by the acceptance of Christ, by the power of the Holy Spirit the instant we accept Christ. Have you been born again? If not, will you take Jesus right now and be born again?

Chapter 7

Refuges of Lies

The hail shall sweep away the refuge of lies.
(Isaiah 28:17)

Every man needs a refuge. Every one of us needs a refuge from four things – the accusations of our own conscience, the power of sin, the displeasure of God, and the wrath to come. Almost every man has something that he is trusting in as a refuge. The trouble is not that men have no refuge, but that they have a false one, what our text characterizes as a *refuge of lies.*

God announced to Israel through His servant Isaiah, and announces to us also, that there is a day coming for testing the refuges of men, and in that day of testing, *the hail shall sweep away the refuge of lies.* Is your refuge a true one or a false one? Is it a refuge that will stand the test of the hour that is coming, or is it a refuge that will go down in a day of storm? Can we tell? We can with absolute certainty.

Four Tests for the Refuge of Lies

There are four commonsense tests that you can apply to every hope that will show clearly whether yours is a true hope or a refuge of lies. First, a true refuge must be one that meets the highest demand of our own conscience. If it does not, it is not a refuge from the accusations of our own conscience, neither is it a refuge from the displeasure of God, for if our own heart condemns us, God is greater than our heart and knows all things.

Second, a true refuge must be one of trust which is making you a better man. If that refuge in which you are trusting is not making you a better man from day to day, it is not a refuge from the power of sin or from the wrath to come. You may rest assured that any hope that does not save you from the power of sin in the present life can never save you from the consequences of sin in the future life.

> A refuge that comforts you when you are strong but fails when you are face-to-face with death is absolutely worthless.

The third test is that a true refuge must stand the test of the dying hour. A refuge that only comforts you when you are well and strong but fails in that dread hour when you are face-to-face with death, God, and eternity is absolutely worthless.

Fourth, a true refuge must be a refuge that will stand the test of the judgment day. Unless it stands that great test, it is powerless. Suppose you had a friend who was under indictment for murder, and you went to see him in the jail before his trial. You find him in a very cheerful frame of mind, and you say to him, "I thought you were under indictment for murder."

And he replies, "I am."

"I thought the trial was near."

"It is."

"Well, you seem to be very cheerful for a man who is under indictment for murder, and whose trial is very near."

"Oh, I am, and the reason is this: I have an answer to make when the trial comes."

"What is your answer? Will it satisfy the judge and jury?"

"No, I don't think it will, but it satisfies me."

"Why," you say, "don't you want to try to defend your case? Your answer is no good unless it will satisfy the judge and jury."

You say you have a refuge that satisfies you. Will it satisfy God? That's the question. Will it satisfy God in the judgment day?

Test Our Own Goodness

Now I am going to apply these four commonsense tests to some of the refuges of lies in which men are trusting today. The first refuge of lies is trust in our own morality, our own goodness, our own character. How many men and women there are who, when you approach them on the subject of becoming a Christian, reply, "No, I don't feel any need of Christ. I am trusting in my own character, in my own daily life. I don't claim to be perfect. Of course, I am not faultless, but I believe that the good in my life will more than counterbalance the evil, and I am trusting in my own good deeds."

Let us apply the tests. Does your goodness meet the highest demand of your own conscience? Be honest now. In all my talking with moralists, and I have talked with a great many, I have only met two men who, when I drove the question home, maintained that their own goodness came up to the highest demand of their own conscience. I have met two. You say that they must have been remarkably good men. No, they had remarkably poor consciences. One of them was a Jew I once met in crossing the Atlantic Ocean. I started to talk to him one day about becoming a Christian, and he said to me, "I feel no need of a Savior."

I said, "Do you mean to tell me that you have never sinned?"

"Never," he said.

"Never fallen below the highest demand of your own conscience?"

"Never."

"Never done anything that you regretted afterwards?"

"Never."

"Well," you say, "he must have been a good man indeed." No, far from it. He was so mean that before we reached New York City, he was the most unpopular man on the ship.

Apply the second test. Is trust in your own goodness making you a better man? As you go on day after day talking about your own morality and trusting in it, do you find, as you grow older, that you are growing more unselfish, more kind, more considerate of others, more helpful, and more humble? I have known many men who trusted in their own morality; I have never known a single one of them who, as he grew older, grew gentler, sweeter, kinder, more considerate of others, and more helpful to his fellow man. Everyone I have known, as they have grown older, has grown more cross, critical, self-centered, and proud.

Apply the third test. Will your own goodness stand the test of the dying hour? How often it does not. How many a man, who in days of health and strength has boasted of his own goodness, but when he comes to his dying bed, has wished that he had a living faith in Christ. In one of my pastorates was perhaps the most self-righteous man I ever knew intimately. He had no use for the church, the Bible, Jesus Christ, ministers, and perhaps most of all, no use for me. He had a particular grudge against me because of something I had once done that he misunderstood, but he was perfectly confident that he was the best man in all the community.

In the passage of time, a cancer appeared on that man's scalp; it spread and ate its way through the scalp until it reached the skull. Then little by little, it ate its way through the skull until there was only a thin film of skull between the cancer and the brain. You could see his brain throbbing beneath the thin film of skull. He knew he would die, and in that hour he said, "Send for Mr. Torrey. I must speak to him." I hurried to his home at once and sat down beside his bed. He said, "Oh, Mr. Torrey, tell me how to be saved. Tell me how to become a Christian."

I took my Bible, and I explained to him just as simply as I knew how what to do to be saved, and I think I can explain it quite simply. But somehow or other he could not grasp it. Hour after hour I sat with him. When night came, I said to his wife and family, "You've been up with him night after night; you are tired, go to bed. I will sit up with him tonight and minister to him." They gave me instructions on what to do and then they retired for the night.

All night long I sat by him, except now and then when I went into the other room to get something for him to eat or drink. Every time when I came back into the room where he was lying in the corner, there came one constant groan from that corner: "Oh, I wish I were a Christian! Oh, I wish I were a Christian! Oh, I wish I were a Christian!" And so the man died. Will it stand the test of the judgment day?

When you stand face-to-face with God, and that fearful, piercing, all-seeing, holy eye looks you through and through, the eye of the One who knows all your past, not only your overt acts but also your covert thoughts, will you look up into His face? Will you say, "O God, Thou Holy One, Thou all-seeing One, You know me through and through; I stand here today confident that my own righteousness will pass with Thee." Never! If you think that you will, go to God tonight and kneel down; look up into God's face and try to tell Him that. You can tell me that, but I don't believe that even you have the brazen arrogance to look up into the face of God and try to tell Him that.

Apply one more test. Will your own goodness stand the test of the Word of God? We know that it will not. We are told in

Galatians 3:10: *As many as are of the works of the law* [who are trying to be saved by their own doings] *are under a curse: for it is written, Cursed is every one who continueth not in all things that are written in the book of the law, to do them.*

And we are told in Romans 3:20 that *by the works of the law shall no flesh be justified in his sight.*

Test the Trusting of Others' Sinfulness
The second refuge of lies is trust in other people's badness. Some people make their boast in their own goodness; others make their boast in the badness of others. How often when you go to a man and urge him to come to Christ, he says, "No, I don't pretend to be very good, but I am just as good as a lot of other folks, just as good as many of your church members."

Let us try that. Does that meet the highest demand of your own conscience? When conscience comes with its domineering demands, does it satisfy your conscience to say, "Well, I am not very good, but I am as good as somebody else." If it does, you must have a mighty mean conscience. Is trust in other people's badness making you a better man? I have known many people who talked much about other people's badness, but I have yet to find the first man or woman who was made better by the process.

> Show me a man that calls every other man a thief, and I will show you a man you can't trust with your pocketbook.

Show me a man who is always talking about the faults of others, and I will show you a man who is rotten at the heart every time. Show me a man that calls every other man a thief, and I will show you a man you can't trust with your pocketbook. Show me a man who thinks every other man is impure, and I will show you an adulterer. Show me a man or woman who is always talking about others' faults, and I will show you a man or woman, without exception, that you can't trust. It never fails.

In one of my pastorates, I had a woman in my Bible class who was in business and was notoriously dishonest. One day she said to me, "Brother Torrey" – oh, she did love the word *brother* – "Brother Torrey, don't you think that everybody in business is dishonest?"

I looked at her and replied, "Mrs. Mac" – she was Scottish – "when anybody in business accuses everybody in business of being dishonest, they convict at least one person." And she was mad! But why should she be mad? I only told her the truth. I made a statement like this in my own church once in an American city: "Show me a person who is always talking about the faults of others, and I will show you a person rotten at the heart."

At the close of the class, a lady in my church came to me and said, "I didn't like something you said this morning."

I said, "What was that?"

"You said, 'Show you a man or woman that was always talking of the faults of others, and you would show them a man or woman rotten at the heart every time.'"

I said, "Yes, I said that, and I meant it too."

"Well," she said, "there is Miss So-and-so; you must admit she is always talking about the faults of others." I had to admit it. "Now," she said, "you would not say she was bad."

Well, I didn't say it, but I could have told this lady that the fact was, earlier that day I had told that woman that she could never sing in our choir again because of awful rottenness in her life that had been brought to my attention. I had charged her with this, and she had confessed. If you know a man or woman who is always talking about the faults of others, don't trust them.

Third, will it stand the test of the dying hour? Never. The time came for his very woman, to whom I have already referred, to die. The physician had done his best. He went into the room and said to her, "Mrs. Mac, it is my duty to tell you I can do no more, neither can any other physician. You will die."

And she shrieked, "Doctor, I can't die! I won't die! I am not ready to die. Doctor, I can't die!" But she did die, and so will you, and in that hour you will not think about the faults of others; rather, the faults of one person will fill the whole horizon, and those are your own faults. Will they stand the test of the judgment day? Face-to-face with God who knows you, will you look up into His face and say, "I have never been good, but I am just as good as others." Never! In that day, God tells us distinctly in Romans 14:12: *Each one of us shall give account of himself to God.*

The Refuge of Universalism

The third refuge of lies is universalism, the belief that God is too good to condemn anyone, and that there is no hell and no future punishment for sin. How common a refuge that is today, and perhaps no more common anywhere than in your city. People respond to you everywhere when you urge them to come to Christ with the answer: "I believe in the mercy of God; I believe in the goodness of God; I believe God is love and too good to condemn anyone. I believe there is no hell and no future punishment."

Let us apply the tests. Does that satisfy the demands of your own conscience? When your conscience points out your sin and demands a change in your life, does it satisfy your conscience to say, "Yes, I know my life is not right, but God is love; therefore, I will continue trampling His laws underfoot, because He is so good and so loving." Is that the kind of conscience you have? If I had that kind of conscience, I would trade it off just as quickly as I could.

Consider this: Here is a boy who has been very ill. He has a loving mother, who loves him enough to die for him if necessary.

Through long days of illness, she will not even hire a nurse, but watches by his bedside until she catches his illness and weakens. Now he is up and around, but she is on the verge of death. She calls him and his sister into the room and says, "Children, I am very low. I may not live the day out, but I want you to go out into the garden into the bright sunshine and enjoy this beautiful day for a while. But Johnnie, when you get out there, you will find some roses in bloom that are the finest. I am saving them for a special purpose. Please don't pluck them, Johnnie."

They go out, and no sooner do they reach the garden than Johnnie begins at once to pluck every one of those roses. Mary says to him, "Johnnie, what are you doing? Didn't you hear what Mother said, that we were not to pull the roses?"

"Oh yes, Mary, I heard her; but Mary, you know how mother loves us. You know how good she is. You know how she watched over me through my illness, how she would not even have a trained nurse, but watched over me herself. Now she is ill today because she loved me and watched over me so tenderly. Mary, that is the reason I am disobeying her, because she loved me so." What would you say of a boy like that?

> You ungrateful men and women are making God's infinite love an excuse for trampling His laws underfoot.

But you contemptible and ungrateful men and women are making God's infinite love that gave His Son to die on the cross of Calvary for you an excuse for trampling His laws underfoot. Shame on you! Don't you ever do it again!

Will your universalism stand the test of the dying hour? A great deal of the universalism of the day does not. Dr. Ichabod Spencer, one of the most celebrated pastors America ever had, wrote a book called *A Pastor's Sketches,* telling of situations from his pastoral work – one of the most valuable books that a minister can possess. One of the sketches is as follows:

In his Brooklyn congregation, there were two married ladies, one the mother-in-law of the other. Neither husband was a Christian. One day the husband of the younger, the son of the older, was taken suddenly and seriously ill. They saw that the illness might result in death, so they sent for Dr. Ichabod Spencer.

When Dr. Spencer came into the room, this young fellow was tossing upon a bed of sickness. Dr. Spencer hurried to his side and tried to present the consolation of the gospel. He said, "Dr. Spencer, I can't listen to you. I have heard it over and over again. I would not listen to it in times of health and strength. I am now very ill. I am dying; I will die soon. I can't repent in this my last hour. I can't do it." And he tossed and groaned in agony upon the bed.

His father was walking up and down the room in great excitement. Finally, he turned to the bed and said, "My son, there is nothing for you to be so anxious about. You have not been a bad boy, and there is no hell. You have nothing to fear."

That dying son turned to his father and said, "Father, you have deceived me all through my life. If I had listened to Mother instead of to you, I would not be here now. She tried to get me to go to church and Sunday school, but you took me off fishing and pleasure-seeking on Sundays. You told me that there was no hell, and I believed you. You have deceived me up to this time, but Father, you can't deceive me any longer. I am dying and going to hell, and my blood is upon your soul." Then he turned his face to the wall and died.

Fathers, you who are spoiling the teaching of godly wives, the day is coming when your sons will curse you. Will your universalism stand the test of the dying hour?

Is it making you a better man? Much of the universalism of the day is not. With many people universalism is simply an excuse for sin! In many of our churches today, the world is sweeping in like a flood! All separation is gone, and professing

Christians are running after the world, the flesh, and the devil because they have accepted the eternal-hope nonsense, which is robbing the church of its devotion and its beauty. They are making the church so like the world that you can't tell the two apart. This universalistic nonsense is simply an excuse for sin – to make men easy in a life of sin and in giving up their separation unto God. Face it squarely; is your universalism making you better men?

Again, will it stand the test of the judgment day? When you meet God face-to-face, will you look into His face and say, "O God, I know my life has not been right, but I thought You were a God of love. I thought You were too good to punish sin. I did not think there was any hell, so I trampled Your laws under-foot." Will you do it? You know you won't.

Refuge of Infidelity
The next refuge of lies is infidelity. How many a man is trying to find comfort in infidelity. Let us apply the tests. Does your infidelity meet the highest demand of your own conscience? When conscience points out your sin and demands a new life, does it satisfy your conscience to say, "Well, I don't believe in the Bible; I don't believe in God. I don't believe that Jesus Christ is the Son of God." Does that satisfy your conscience? If it does, you are not fit to be called a human being.

Is your infidelity making you a better man? I have known many unbelievers. My ministry has been largely a ministry to skeptics, agnostics, and infidels. I have had their confidence, and I have yet to meet the first infidel that was made better by infidelity. I have known men whose characters have been undermined by infidelity – countless men. I have had young men come to me with breaking hearts, with saddest confessions of immorality and of ruin, and I have had them say to me time and again, "The first step was listening to Colonel Ingersoll," or some other infidel lecturer or reading an infidel book.

I tell you, men, young men especially, who are trifling with infidelity: you are undermining the foundations of sound character. Infidelity is sowing the world with wickedness. In my own church one night in Chicago, to which many unbelievers come, one of them said to me, "We come over here to hear you. You don't spare us, but we like men to stand up to the rack. That is the reason we come."

There are always a lot of them every Sunday. Thank God, many of them are converted, so we like to see them come. They are very friendly and very kind. When we left Chicago, I think the person that came nearest to breaking into tears was the wife of one of the most notorious infidels in Chicago. She was an infidel herself, or tried to be. But now for my story:

One night in my church in Chicago, I said, "I would like to put this thing to the test. I would like to ask every man in this congregation who has been saved from drunkenness by Jesus Christ and the Bible to stand up." All over that building about two hundred men stood up, indicating they were saved from drunkenness by the Bible and Christ. I said, "That will do. Now I am going to be fair. I would like to ask every man in this audience who has been saved from drunkenness or any other definite sin by infidelity in any form to stand up." I thought that no one had risen, but finally as I looked over that great crowd, a ways off under the gallery, I saw one man standing – a poor, seedy-looking negro, the only man in the audience who had been saved from drunkenness or other sin by infidelity; he was drunk at the time, but he had sense enough to come to Christ at the close of the meeting.

Infidelity makes nobody a better man.

Men, face facts. Infidelity makes nobody a better man. Will it stand the test of the dying hour? How often it fails. A friend of mine who was in the Northern Army in the Civil War said that in the same company with him was a man who was a loud-spoken infidel, who loved to talk a great deal in the camp. On the second day of the battle of Pittsburg Landing, he said to the boys in the morning, "Boys, it seems as if I will be shot today."

"Oh," they said, "nonsense. It is nothing but superstition. You are not going to be shot."

"Well," he said, "I feel very strange. I feel as if I am going to be shot."

At last they were lined up waiting for the word of command. "Forward, march!" Up they went to the top of the hill, and as they reached the crest of the hill, a burst came from the enemy's guns. At the very first gunfire, a bullet pierced this man near the heart, and as he fell back into the arms of the comrade behind him, he threw his hands in the air and cried as they carried him to the rear, "Oh God, just give me time to repent." It only took one bullet to take the infidelity out of that man. It would take less than that to take the nonsense out of most of you.

Will infidelity stand the test of the judgment day? Will you go into God's presence and be ready to say, "Oh God, my answer is this: I was an infidel, an agnostic, a skeptic, an atheist, and a materialist." Do you think you will? I will tell you how to put it to the test. Go alone tonight, get down on your knees, and try to tell Him. You can talk nonsense to your fellow man, but when you talk to God, it will take the nonsense out of you.

One night I went into the audience to speak to individuals after a meeting like this. I went to a man who sat in the last opera chair. I said to him, "Are you a Christian?"

"No," he said, "I should say not. I am an infidel."

I said, "What do you mean?"

"Well," he said, "I don't believe in the divinity of Christ."

I said, "You don't believe in the divinity of Christ?"

"No," he said, "I don't."

"Well," I said, "let us kneel down right now and tell God so." And he turned pale. You go and tell God what you would like to tell me.

Refuge of Religion

One more refuge of lies is hypocritical religion. You say, "What! Religion? You don't mean what you say." I mean every word, if it is religion of a hypocritical sort. I say religion in and of itself is often just as much a refuge of lies as morality, other people's badness, universalism, and infidelity. Religious activities by themselves never saved anybody. It is one thing to trust in religion; it is something entirely different to trust in a living Christ. How many men are making their boast in their hypocritical religion. People say, "Oh, I am very religious. I go to church. I say my prayers every morning and night. I read my Bible. I go to Communion. I have been baptized. I have been confirmed. I give a tenth of my income to the poor. I am very religious."

Well, you can do every bit of that and go straight to hell. Others say, "I make my confession on Saturday and attend Mass on Sunday; I say many 'Our Fathers' and 'Hail Marys'; I count my beads and sprinkle myself with holy water." You can do it all and go straight to hell. Religion itself never saved anybody.

Apply the tests. Is your religion making you a better man or woman? Much religion doesn't make men or women one bit better. Some people say prayers, read the Bible, go to church, talk in meetings, and are very prominent in the church, but they will lie as fast as anybody. Many people who do all these things will go around slandering their neighbors. Many men who are religious and very prominent in the church will deceive you in a business deal as much as any man in town. Many a man who is religious treats his servants like brutes and oppresses his employees. Many religious men turn a deaf ear to the cry of the widow and the orphan, unless their generosity will be reported in the papers. Many a man is religious but a perfect scoundrel.

I met a man in this country; he seemed to be a most religious man. I met him one Sunday morning. He said, "I am going to conduct a meeting," and he had dressed himself to look as much like a preacher as he could. He made his employees gather at a certain hour every day for prayer, and he held a religious service with them every Sunday, so that they would not have to go to church. I was informed of the wages that this pious humbug was paying the girls who worked for him. They were starvation wages. I saw the girls, and they were the palest, most pinched crowd of girls I have seen in all England; man after man told me how he tried to get the better of them in deals. That kind of religion will send a man to the deepest hell there is.

In the second place, will your religion stand the test of the dying hour? Much religion doesn't. Many very active religious people are as scared as anybody when they come to die. Oh, how I have heard them groan and sigh and weep in the dying hour. Their hollow religion doesn't stand the test of that great crisis.

Will it stand the test of the judgment day? Mere religion will not, for the Lord Jesus Christ Himself says, *Many will say to me in that day, Lord, Lord, did we not prophesy by thy name, and by thy name cast out demons, and by thy name do many mighty works? And then will I profess unto them, I never knew you: depart from me, ye that work iniquity* (Matthew 7:22-23).

Religion is a refuge of lies, and if that is what you are trusting in, you are lost forever unless you get something better.

Well, someone will say, is there no true refuge? There is. It is found in the verse before my text. God says, *Behold, I lay in Zion for a foundation a stone, a tried stone, a precious cornerstone of sure foundation: he that believeth shall not be in haste* (Isaiah 28:16).

That sure foundation stone is Jesus Christ. *Other foundation can no man lay than that which is laid, which is Jesus Christ* (1 Corinthians 3:11).

It is one thing to trust in religion, and something entirely different to trust in a crucified and risen Christ with a living faith. Will that refuge stand the test of our own conscience? It will, thank God. When my conscience points to my sin, I have an answer that satisfies it, and that answer is Jesus, who bore my sins in His own body on the cross. Will it make men better men? Yes. A living faith in a crucified and living Christ will make every man who has it more and more like Christ every day of his life, and if you have a faith that is not making you like Christ, you don't have a real faith.

Whosoever believeth that Jesus is the Christ is begotten of God: and . . . whosoever is begotten of God overcometh the world (1 John 5:1, 4). If the world is overcom-

> When my conscience points to my sin, I have an answer that satisfies it, and that answer is Jesus.

ing you, you don't have a living, saving faith in the Son of God. Will it stand the test of the dying hour? Thank God, yes. How often I have gone to a dying bed and looked men, women, and children in the face and said to them, "My brother, my sister, your time is short. Before morning breaks you will have passed into the great beyond."

And with a calm, triumphant, and ecstatic voice, they said, "I know it; I am ready to go."

The happiest scenes I have ever seen on earth have been deathbed scenes of true Christians – scenes of triumph and glory. One day at the close of my Bible class in Chicago, the president of the class came up to me and said, "Pomeroy" (one of the members of my class) "is dying of tuberculosis. I don't think he will live until morning. I know you are busy, but can't you go and see him?"

I said, "Certainly, Fred." I went and found him propped

up with pillows. I said to him, "Mr. Pomeroy, they tell me you can't live through the night."

"Oh," he said, "I know."

I said, "Are you afraid to die?"

"Afraid?" he said. "Afraid to die? No, I shall be glad to depart and be with Christ." How often I have seen this.

Will it stand the test of the judgment day? Yes, if it is God's will. I say that reverently and thoughtfully – if it is the will of God, I am willing to face God tonight in judgment.

You say, "What, have you never sinned?"

Alas! I have. Thank God, you will never know how deeply I have sinned. But when God asks for an answer, I will say one word – *Jesus* – and that will satisfy God. It already satisfies me. That response will sweep away every refuge of lies. Throw them all away and come to Christ; be ready for life, ready for death, and ready for eternity.

Chapter 8

Found Out

Be sure your sin will find you out. (Numbers 32:23)

No man can escape his own sins. Every sin we commit will find us out and call us to account and make us pay. No man ever committed a single sin that he did not pay for in some way. No man ever committed a single sin by which he was not a loser. The utmost foolishness that a man can be guilty of is for him to imagine he can gain something by doing wrong. Whether you hurt another by your own wrongdoing or not, you are bound to hurt yourself.

There are doubtless many people who contemplate doing some wrong act. Very likely you could be thinking about doing it tonight. I want to say to you now, as Moses said to the children of Reuben and Gad, *Be sure your sin will find you out.* You can't escape it, and you are bound to suffer from that sin. It is most likely that if a man puts his hand in the fire, he will be burned. It is absolutely sure that if a man sins, he will suffer for it and suffer for each individual sin he commits. You may escape the law, but you cannot escape the consequences of your own sins.

You may escape the laws of men, but you cannot escape the law of God. No man can hide where his sin will not find him. Here are six ways in which a man's sins find him out.

By the Execution of Human Laws

The execution of laws in human society is imperfect, and yet it is astonishing how men who break the laws are sooner or later brought to accountability. A man may elude the maze of the law for days, weeks, months, or years, but he is always weaving a net that will entrap him in the end. Here is an illustration. Some years ago a crime was committed in the city of Chicago. The detectives set to work to ferret out the criminal. Every clue failed. One day a detective was speaking to me about it. We were just about to separate. He was utterly discouraged. At the last moment, a thought flashed through my mind about someone who had not once been suspected. The man had supposedly covered all his tracks, and not a soul on earth but himself knew that he was the criminal. Within two hours, that person was under arrest and had made full confession of his crime. It is a marvelous thing how crime comes to light and how a man's sin finds him out and exposes him to the contempt of the whole world.

An intimate connection exists between morality and health.

In Our Own Bodies

When a man does not pay the penalty for his sin before human courts, he pays for it in a court where there is no possibility of bribery – the court of physical retribution for moral offenses. Not only do certain diseases emerge from certain sins, but also in a general way an intimate connection exists between morality and health. All sins have physical consequences. The suffering that results from some sins is not as immediate or as marked as the physical suffering that results from a few well-known vices, but it is still true that every sin has physical consequences. The man who sins will suffer for it in his body. His sin is bound to find him out.

Scarcely a week passes that someone does not come to me, suffering some great physical evil that is simply the consequence of his own sin. Young men see others suffering the terrible consequences of transgressing God's law, but they still go right on as an ox to the slaughter. They think that they will be an exception, but there are no exceptions to physical law. Any action that is unnatural or immoral is bound to bring a penalty.

Why are there so many men with broken bodies and shattered intellects? Because of a violation of God's law – their sin has found them out. Why are there so many broken-down women? Because of a violation of God's law – your sins are finding you out. Of course, disease may be hereditary or the result of accident or misfortune, but if we could eliminate all the sickness that is the result directly or indirectly of our own sin, we would be surprised at the small amount of sickness that would be left.

Many excellent young men have been guilty of certain sins, and the body is shattered, and the mind diminished as a consequence. The same is true of many young women who in many other respects are most admirable young women. Consider even such a sin as anger. Does that affect a man's body? Surely. It disorders his blood, stomach, brain, and nerves. It is demonstrably unhealthy in every case, and can even lead to paralysis and death.

In one church where I was pastor, one of the deacons had a stroke with paralysis that finally resulted in death. It was said that the stroke was due to this excellent man losing his temper in a political discussion. It is simply astounding, if you study it, the many ways – some simple, some intricate, some direct and some indirect – in which our sins hunt us down and find us out in our own bodies. Man, if you are contemplating sin, just stop and think of this for a moment: *Be sure your sin will find you out*! If nowhere else, in that body of yours, you will in some measure pay a physical penalty for every sin you commit.

In Our Character

Our sin finds us out in another place, and this is more important by far than its finding us out in the execution of human laws or its finding us out in our bodies. Sin finds us out in our character. For every sin you commit, you will suffer in character. Every sin breeds a moral ulcer. A festering body is not as bad as a festering character. You can't tell a lie without your moral blood being poisoned by it and your moral constitution being undermined.

Do you think you can cheat a man in business and not suffer in your character more than he suffers in his pocket? Do you think that you can wrong an employee in his wages and not suffer more in what you become than the loss he suffers? Do you think you can wrong a man regarding his wife and not have a death-dealing cancer in your own character? Do you think you can read an impure book or tell or listen to an obscene story and not breed a stinking distemper in your own moral nature? Do you think you can violate those laws of purity that God has written in His Word, on your heart, and in your body and not reap disgusting tumors in your own character? Wherever else the law may seem to fail, it absolutely never fails here. A man's sin, a

> For every sin you commit, you will suffer in character.

woman's sin, always finds them out in their character – in what they themselves become.

In Our Own Conscience

From whomever else you can hide your sin, you cannot hide it from yourself. You are so constructed in the mercy of God that to know you are a sinner means self-condemnation and agony. How many of you are suffering untold agonies from the bitter consciousness of sins that no one knows anything about but you? No physical torments match the torments of an accusing conscience. An accusing conscience means hell on earth. No earthly prosperity, no human love, no mirth nor music, no revelry, fun, or intoxication can dispel its clouds or soothe the agony of its ever-gnawing tooth. The old Latin poet Juvenal put it well:

> Trust me, no tortures that the poets feign
> Can match the fierce, unutterable pain
> He feels, who night and day, devoid of rest,
> Carries his own accuser in his breast.

There is a place where all our sins will soon find us out – every one of us. Have no doubt of that, my friend. *Be sure your sin will find you out.* It may be hidden from the officer of the law; it may be hidden from the eye of every man and every woman; but it will speak to your conscience someday. It will find you there; then beware! That sin you are considering looks fair and sweet. It won't look so fair, nor taste so sweet, after it is committed. It will find you out, and you will suffer. Oh, how you will suffer!

Before we move on, let me say that the fact that your sin is sure to find you out in so many ways – in your relationships to your fellow man, in your body, in your character, and in your conscience – all points unmistakably to the existence of a moral governor of this universe. Everything in this universe is tuned to virtue. The stars in their courses fight against Sisera. Everything conspires to punish sin and reward goodness. To see this and to question the existence of such a God as the Bible pictures is to be supremely irrational.

In Our Children

There is another place where *your sin will find you out* – in your children. That is one of the worst things about sin; its curse falls not only upon us but upon our children also. God does visit the iniquities of the fathers upon the children. You may complain about that as much as you like, but it is an unquestionable fact; a wise man doesn't think as much of what he would like to have true as of what really is true. There is no question that our sins find us out in our children.

Let a man be a drinking man, for example. He may not be a very hard drinker, but there is almost sure to be a curse upon his children. Most likely one of his sons will be a drunkard. I remember a man who was a constant but moderate drinker. He had three sons. I don't think that man was ever drunk in his life. Indeed, he despised a drunkard, but he laughed at total abstainers. Each one of his three sons became a drunkard.

In a New England town, I knew of a young woman who belonged to one of the best families. I don't think her father was a drunkard, but he was a moderate drinker; the daughter, however, inherited an appetite that completely overcame her. She became a periodical drunkard. At times she would disappear from home and go to Boston; when pursued, she was found in the lowest slums, beastly drunk. Her father's sin had found him out.

Consider the liquor dealer. His sin is almost sure to find him out in his children. A friend of mine who has wide experience says he never knew a man in the liquor business where the curse did not sooner or later strike in his own home. A man was pointed out to me in an American town as the one who had made a determined effort to upset the temperance principles of the majority of the town by opening a saloon. Two members of his own family came to violent deaths through drink. His sin found him out.

Consider the Sabbath-breaker. Today many Christians are careless about the Lord's Day. They go out riding to the park, bicycling, or playing golf. Let them beware. Their sin will find them out in their children. Their children will go farther than they do. They will disregard the day altogether; they will likely turn out to be infidels, drunkards and perverts, and all that is bad.

The one thing I thank God for in my home training is the strictness with which we were trained to observe the Lord's Day. Some of us wandered into sin in later life, but when that one day in seven came around, we couldn't find the heart to do what we did on other days. We would go to church, and so we were brought back to Christ.

The sin of the adulterer will find him out in his own children. Let him take heed regarding his daughter. A very prominent man in America, an excellent man in many respects, was led into sin. Very few knew of it, but his wife knew and freely forgave him. But his sin found him out in his own family. His own daughter fell prey to an infamous scoundrel. You who are considering some sinful act, beware, lest you bring a curse upon your own household. It looks attractive now. It seems as if it would be convenient, but it won't. *Be sure your sin will find you out.*

In Eternity

Your sin will find you out in one more place – in eternity. This present life is not all there is. A future life exists, and our acts and their consequences will follow us into it. If your sin does not find you out here, it will there. You may be sure of that. In eternity we shall reap the consequences of every sin we sow. This sometimes seems to go on, unchecked by justice. Men defraud their employees; they rob the widow and the orphan; they condemn other men and their families to poverty in order to increase their already too-enormous wealth, and no one seems to call them to account.

It will not always be so. God will call them to account, to strict account, and a few thousands, or hundreds of thousands, or millions of their ill-gotten wealth given to charity will not blind the eyes of a holy God. They will suffer. Men sometimes lay traps for foolish girls, and they are ruined, and no one seems to call the men to account. They go on and on, admitted to the "best society," and loaded with honors. It will not always be so. Their sin will find them out, if not in this world, in the next; they will stand before the universe exposed in shame, loaded with dishonor, and cast out to everlasting contempt.

Men despise God, laugh at His Word, and trample underfoot His Son, and God still lets them live. He does not seem to call them to account. But it will not always be so. *Be sure your sin will find you out.*

> *At the revelation of the Lord Jesus from heaven with*
> *the angels of his power in flaming fire, rendering*
> *vengeance to them that know not God, and to them*
> *that obey not the gospel of our Lord Jesus: who shall*
> *suffer punishment, even eternal destruction from*
> *the face of the Lord and from the glory of his might*
> (2 Thessalonians 1:7-8).

Be sure your sin will find you out. The principle of our text is sure. All history is a confirmation of and commentary on this point of the Word of God. Every man's experience is a confirmation of it. You cannot sin without suffering for it. Your sin will find you out in the workings of human society, in your own body, in your character, in your conscience, in your children, in eternity, or in all of these. Are you considering sin now? Don't do it. I beg of you, don't do it. You will regret it. You will suffer; you will pay an awful price. *Your sin will find you out.*

You cannot sin without suffering for it.

But many of us have sinned already, and our sins are finding us out already. What shall we do? Fly to Christ. I have preached law to you. Now, a word of gospel. There is but one way to escape the penalties of the law – that is, in the grace of the gospel. *Christ redeemed us from the curse of the law, having become a curse for us* (Galatians 3:13).

Fly to Him at once. He calls, *Come unto me, all ye that labor and are heavy laden, and I will give you rest* (Matthew 11:28). Come – come at once.

Chapter 9

Who Then Can Be Saved?

Then who can be saved? (Mark 10:26)

The disciples asked Jesus that question. He had just told them how hard it was for a rich man to enter into the kingdom of heaven, and the disciples seem to have held the same opinion as most men hold today – that a rich man can get anywhere. But Jesus said no; it was easier for a camel to pass through the eye of a needle than for a rich man to enter the kingdom of God. Then they asked the question: If that is so – if it is so hard for a rich man to be saved – what chance does anyone else have?

Then who can be saved? Jesus told them that it was impossible with men for a rich man to be saved; the rich man stands the poorest chance of salvation of anybody on earth. There are fewer rich people saved than people of any other class. Jesus told them that God, with whom all things are possible, could save even a rich man, but nobody except God could do this.

We come, then, to the question itself: *Then who can be saved?* The Bible answers the question fully and plainly. The Bible tells us that there are some people who cannot be saved, and that there are some people who can be saved.

Who Cannot Be Saved?

In the first place, no man can be saved who will not give up his sin. We read in Isaiah 55:7: *Let the wicked forsake his way, and the unrighteous man his thoughts: and let him return unto the* LORD, *and he will have mercy upon him; and to our God, for he will abundantly pardon.* But if he will not forsake his ways and turn to God, he cannot be saved. Every man and every woman has to choose between sin and salvation. You cannot have both. If you won't give up sin, you must give up salvation. *Not everyone who says to me, 'Lord, Lord,' will enter the kingdom of heaven, but only the one who does the will of my Father who is in heaven* (Matthew 7:21).

There are schemes of salvation that propose salvation for a man while he continues in sin. These schemes are absurdities. We read in Matthew 1:21, concerning our Savior: *Thou shalt call his name JESUS; for it is he that shall save his people from their sins. From* their sins, not *in* them. You cannot save a man while he continues in sin. Sin is damnation; holiness is salvation. And you might as well propose to cure a man who is ill while he continues in his disease as to save a sinner while he continues in his sin. A man is not cured until he is well, and a man is not saved until he quits sin.

Sin is damnation; holiness is salvation.

The reason some of you are not saved is that you won't give up sin. Some of you won't give up your drunkenness; some of you won't give up your adultery; some of you won't give up your profanity; some of you won't give up your lying; some of you won't give up your bad temper; some won't give up one thing, and some won't give up another. Well, then, you must go into hell. You cannot be saved if you won't give up sin, and if you persist in sinning you will be lost forever.

A man in Chicago came to a friend of mine and said, "I want to be saved."

My friend replied, "You do not want to be saved."

"But," he said, "I do."

My friend said, "You are not willing to give up your drinking."

"No," he said, "I am not."

"Well, then, you do not want to be saved. To be repent means to give up sin." Jesus Christ can save any man, but Jesus Christ won't; He can't save a man who won't give up his sin. *Except ye repent, ye shall all likewise perish* (Luke 13:5).

In the second place, no man can be saved who trusts in his own righteousness and is not willing to admit that he is a lost sinner. That is the trouble with many of you. You are proud of your own morality; you are not willing to get down to the dust and say, "I am a poor, vile, worthless, miserable sinner." You will never be saved and never can be saved while you trust in your own righteousness.

Jesus tells us that two men went up to the temple to pray; one was a Pharisee, one of the most respectable, religious men in the community, a man that everybody looked up to; the other was a publican, a man that everybody looked down upon. The Pharisee prayed this way: He talked about his own goodness. He looked up and said, *God, I thank thee, that I am not as the rest of men, extortioners, unjust, adulterers* [and then he looked contemptuously over to the poor publican], *or even as this publican. I fast twice in the week* [quite religious, wasn't he?]; *I give tithes of all that I get* (Luke 18:11-12).

And Jesus said that this man went out of the temple down to his house an unforgiven, lost sinner; but the publican, the outcast, the man that everybody looked down upon, would not so much as lift up his eyes to heaven. He felt he was a miserable, worthless sinner. He beat upon his breast, and said, *God, be thou merciful to me a sinner* (Luke 18:13). And Jesus said that *this man went down to his house justified.* Anybody can be saved who will take the sinner's place and cry for mercy; nobody else can.

I have a quaint friend who is Scottish; one day he was walking through the country when a man came along in a carriage. He saw the old man walking and invited him to get into the carriage, which he very promptly did, for he saw an opportunity for doing good. The man who had invited him into the carriage was curious to know who the old Scotsman was, so he asked him questions. Finally, the old Scotsman said, "I will tell you who I am, and I will tell you what my business is. I have a very strange business. I am hunting for heirs."

The other man said, "What?"

"I am hunting for heirs – heirs to a great estate. I represent a very great estate, and I am hunting for heirs for it; there are many around this neighborhood."

The other said, "Do you mind telling me their names?"

"No," he said, "it is a very large family; their name begins with S."

"Oh," said the man, "Smith, I suppose?"

"No," the old man replied, "a much larger family than the Smith family."

He says, "Larger than the Smith family! Who are they?"

The old Scotsman said, "They are the sinner family. The estate I represent is the kingdom of God, *an inheritance incorruptible, and undefiled, and that fadeth not away* (1 Peter 1:4), and the heirs to it are the sinners who are willing to take the family name, admit that they are sinners, and look to God for pardon."

Do you belong to that family? Do you belong to the sinner family? If you do, you can be saved. If you are not willing to admit that you do, you cannot be saved. You are lost forever.

In the third place, no man or woman can be saved who

is not willing to accept salvation as a free gift. We are told in Ephesians 2:8: *For by grace have ye been saved through faith; and that not of yourselves, it is the gift of God.* Romans 6:23 tells us *the free gift of God is eternal life in Christ Jesus our Lord.* Salvation is a free gift. Anybody can have it. If you are not willing to take it as a free gift, you cannot have it at all.

My wife was talking one day to a young man, a son of the richest man in the neighborhood. There seemed to be some difficulty about his accepting Christ. Finally, my wife said to him, calling him by his name, "The trouble with you is you are not willing to accept salvation as a free gift."

He said, "Mrs. Torrey, that is just it; I am not willing to accept salvation as a free gift. If I could earn it, if I could work for it, if I could deserve it, I would. I am willing to earn it, but I am not willing to take it as a free gift."

Well, nobody can earn it; nobody can work for it; nobody can deserve it; nobody can get it except for nothing; and unless you are willing to take it as a free gift, you will never get it at all. The richest millionaire has to get it the same way as the pauper – as a free gift; the richest man on earth who gets saved will **Anybody can be saved in Christ; nobody can be saved in any other way.** have nothing more to boast of when he gets to heaven than the poorest pauper who is saved.

Fourth, nobody can be saved who will not accept Jesus Christ as his Savior. We are told in Acts 4:12: *Neither is there any other name under heaven, that is given among men, wherein we must be saved.* Anybody can be saved in Christ; nobody can be saved in any other way. An infidel once said to a friend of mine, Mr. Henry Varley, "If I cannot be saved without accepting Christ, I won't be saved." Well, then, he won't be saved. That is all there is to it; he won't be saved.

If you should ever go to Sydney, you will soon discover that every citizen in the city is proud of their harbor. You won't be in Sydney half an hour before somebody will ask you, "What do you think of our harbor?" They may well be proud of it. It is one of the finest, if not *the* finest, harbor in the world – beautiful and spacious. But it has only one entrance. There is one high promontory of rock called the North Head and another high promontory called the South Head, and the only channel, which is wide and deep, is between these two heads.

A short distance south of the South Head is another bluff called Jacob's Ladder. One night, many years ago, a vessel called the *Duncan Dunbar,* with hundreds of people on board, came outside of Sydney Harbour after dark. The captain saw the South Head and thought it was the North Head; he saw Jacob's Ladder and thought it was the South Head. He steered and advanced full speed; he steamed in between the two lights and ran onto the rocks, and every one of the hundreds on board perished, except one man who was thrown up into a cave on the face of the rock.

Now, that captain was perfectly sincere. There never was a more sincere man on earth, but he was mistaken, and he was lost. People say it does not make any difference what you believe if you are only sincere, but the more sincerely you believe error, the worse off you are. There is just one channel into salvation, and that is Christ. Try to go any other way, no matter how sincere you are, and you will be wrecked and lost eternally.

Who Can Be Saved?

First, sinners can be saved, even the vilest. We read in 1 Timothy 1:15: *Faithful is the saying, and worthy of all acceptation, that Christ Jesus came into the world to save sinners; of whom I am chief.* He has already saved the chief of sinners, and He is able to do it again.

In Minneapolis, where I used to live, a young girl of thirteen was seduced. Her father and mother cast her off – all the more shame for them. Her brothers cast her off, and I doubt they were any better than she was, but it is one thing for a girl to sin and another thing for a man to sin. In the eyes of man, it is worse for the girl, but it is not so in the eyes of God. They cast off this poor girl of only thirteen years of age, and I think they were worse than she was – more devilish. Of course, she transgressed; she became the companion of thieves, robbers, forgers, and murderers. She participated in everything that was disreputable and became a member of two of the worst gangs at different times in New York and Chicago.

One night when she had plummeted into sin, a friend of mine met her and said to her, "If you are ever sick of this life, come to me, and I will help you out of it." A night came when she was thoroughly sick of it, and she went to this gentleman's house – a very wealthy man, who used his money for God. He was one rich man who was saved, but he had given most of his money away. She went to his house. His wife tried to show her the way of life. After a while the gentleman came in and showed her the way of life, and she was saved.

Today that young woman occupies a high position of great responsibility and honor in America, and almost no one in society where she is a high officer even knows of her past life. God has covered it up, though she bears the same name as she did in that life. A few years ago, I was in Northfield, and she came to me and said, "I hope, Mr. Torrey, that you won't think it necessary to tell the people here." (Mrs. Torrey and I were about the only ones who knew her past record; she had been in our house in the days of her trouble.) "I hope you won't think it necessary to tell the people here my story."

I said, "Most assuredly we shall not," for why should you tell a saved woman's story, when it is covered by the blood, anymore than a saved man's story? It is no longer her story; it is blotted out. And that woman is today a highly honored woman. Out of the deepest depth of sin, Jesus Christ has not only saved her but also covered up her past.

In the second place, any man or woman who is too weak to resist sin in their own strength can be saved. It is not a question of your strength but of Christ's strength. We read in Jude 1:24: *Now unto him that is able to guard you from stumbling, and to set you before the presence of his glory without blemish in exceeding joy.* We read in 1 Peter 1:5: *Who by the power of God are guarded through faith unto a salvation.* Jesus Christ can keep the weakest man or woman just as well as the strongest.

> **Jesus Christ can keep the weakest man or woman just as well as the strongest.**

I have seen men start out in the Christian life who talk like this in testimony meetings: "Friends, you know me; I am a man of great decision of character. When I make up my mind to do anything, I always follow through. I have started out in this Christian life, and I want you to understand that I am not going to backslide as so many do; I am following through."

Whenever I hear a man talking that way, I know he is going to backslide within six weeks. Another man will stand up trembling and hesitant, and he will say, "You all know me; you know I have no willpower left; I have tried to quit my sin, time and again, and as you know, I have failed every time. I have absolutely no confidence in myself, but God says in Isaiah 41:10, *Fear thou not, for I am with thee; be not dismayed, for I am thy God; I will strengthen thee; yea, I will help thee; yea, I will uphold thee with the right hand of my righteousness,* and I am trusting in Him." When I hear a man talking that way, I know he is going to stand every time.

One day some people came to me in Chicago and said, "We must find a place for Mrs. S."

I said, "Why?"

"Well," they said, "Nels got drunk last night and tried to kill his wife with a shoe knife, and it is not safe for her nor her child, so she has left her husband. We must do something to provide for her."

I said, "You are quite right to provide for her; that is what we ought to do."

Not long after, Nels came to me and said, "Mr. Torrey, do you know where my wife is?"

I said, "I do."

He said, "Will you please tell me where she is?"

I replied, "I will not. You tried to kill her; you are a brute; you do not deserve to have a wife, and I am not going to tell you where she is to let you go and kill her."

He said, "If you do not tell me, I will commit suicide."

"Very well," I said. "You will go to hell if you do."

That kind of fellow never commits suicide. He kept getting drunk. He could not help it, poor fellow. Every little while he would come to me for five cents or for ten cents, saying that he was going to get a job in a shoe factory. I always knew that the money was going for whiskey. He got many five-cent pieces from me, and from many of my students; the money always went for whiskey. Years and years went by, and Nels always said that he was going to quit drinking. I knew he was not. He meant to. He would come, saying that he was hunting for work, but I knew he was looking for another drink.

That went on for years. One day I said to God, "Heavenly Father, if you will give me Nels S., I will never despair of another man as long as I live." I do not know if it was the same week, but I am sure it was very soon after that, that Nels got his feet upon the Rock, Christ Jesus, and never fell again.

Years have passed; he is an honored member of my church. When I was home this summer, among those who came to welcome me was Nels, his wife, and his child – a happy family in Jesus Christ.

The Christ who saved Nels, the lying, habitual, hopeless drunkard, can save any man or woman who will trust Him.

Third, any man can be saved who thinks he has committed the unpardonable sin, but who is willing to come to Jesus Christ now. Jesus says in John 6:37, *Him that cometh to me I will in no wise cast out.* I think I have never gone to any place in my life where somebody has not written to me or come to me and said, "I have committed the unpardonable sin," and almost every one, if not every one, has gone away rejoicing in Jesus Christ. I get letters every week from all over England from people who tell me that they have committed the unpardonable sin.

> Any man can be saved who thinks he has committed the unpardonable sin, but who is willing to come to Jesus Christ now.

One time I received a letter from a brokenhearted father who was a Presbyterian minister. He wrote that he had a son who was in spiritual darkness. The son thought that he had committed the unpardonable sin, and he was plunged into absolute despair. Would I take him at the Bible institute? I replied that though I had sympathy with him in his sorrow, the Bible institute was not designed to help cases like these but to train men and women for Christian service.

The father continued to write, begging me to take his son; he even got other friends to plead for him. Finally, I consented to take the young man. He was sent to me under guard, lest he do some rash thing along the way.

When he was brought to my office, I showed him to a seat. As soon as the others had left the room, he began the conversation by saying, "I am possessed by the devil."

"I think quite likely you are," I replied, "but Christ is able to cast out devils."

"You do not understand me," he said. "I mean that the devil has entered into me as he did into Judas Iscariot."

"That may be," I answered, "but Christ came to destroy the works of the devil. Now He says in John 6:37, *Him that cometh to me I will in no wise cast out.* If you will just come to Him, He will receive you and set you free from Satan's power."

The conversation went on in this way for some time – he constantly asserting the absolute hopelessness of his case and me constantly asserting the power of Jesus Christ and His promise: *Him that cometh to me I will in no wise cast out.* After a while, I sent the young man to his room.

Days and weeks passed, and we had many conversations, always along the same line; I always held him to John 6:37. One day I met him in the hall of the institute and made up my mind that the time had come to have the battle out. I told him to sit down, and I sat down beside him. "Do you believe the Bible?" I asked.

"Yes," he replied, "I believe everything in it."

"Do you believe John 6:37?" I asked.

"Yes, I believe everything in the Bible."

"Do you believe that Jesus Christ told the truth when He said, *Him that cometh to me I will in no wise cast out*?"

"Yes, I do; I believe everything in the Bible."

"Well, then, will you come?"

"I have committed the unpardonable sin."

I replied, "Jesus does not say, 'Him that hath not committed the unpardonable sin that cometh to Me, I will in no wise cast out.' He says, *Him that cometh to me I will in no wise cast out.*"

"But I have sinned willfully after I have received the knowledge of the truth."

"Jesus does not say, 'Him that has not sinned willfully after he received the knowledge of the truth that cometh unto Me, I will in no wise cast out.' He says, *Him that cometh to me I will in no wise cast out.*"

"But I have once been enlightened and have tasted the heavenly gift and have fallen away; it is impossible to renew me again unto repentance."

"Jesus does not say, 'Him that has not tasted of the heavenly gift and has not fallen away, if he cometh to Me I will in no wise cast him out.' He says, *Him that cometh to me I will in no wise cast out.*"

"But I am possessed of the devil," he answered.

"Jesus does not say, 'Him that is not possessed of the devil that cometh to Me I will in no wise cast out.' He says, *Him that cometh to me I will in no wise cast out.*"

"I mean that the devil has entered into me, as he did into Judas Iscariot."

"Jesus does not say, 'Him that the devil has not entered into, as he did into Judas Iscariot, that cometh to Me, I will in no wise cast out.' He says, *Him that cometh to me I will in no wise cast out.*"

"But my heart is as hard as a millstone."

"Jesus does not say, 'If a man's heart is soft and tender, and he comes unto Me, I will in no wise cast him out.' He says, *Him that cometh to me I will in no wise cast out.*"

"But I do not know that I have any desire to come."

"Jesus does not say, 'Him that hath a desire to come and comes unto Me, I will in no wise cast out.' He says, *Him that cometh to Me I will in no wise cast out.*"

"But I do not know that I can come in the right way."

"Jesus does not say, 'Him that cometh to Me in the right way, I will in no wise cast him out.' He says, *Him that cometh to me I will in no wise cast out.*"

"Well, I don't know that I care to come."

"Jesus does not say, 'Him that cares to come to Me and comes to Me, I will in no wise cast out.' He says, *Him that cometh to me I will in no wise cast out.*"

The man's excuses and evasions were exhausted. I looked him squarely in the face and said, "Now, will you come? Get down on your knees and quit your nonsense." He knelt, and I knelt by his side. "Now," I said, "follow me in prayer."

"Lord Jesus, my heart is as hard as a millstone" I said.

He repeated, "Lord Jesus, my heart is as hard as a millstone."

"I have no desire to come to You, but You have said in Your Word, *Him that cometh to me I will in no wise cast out.*"

"I have no desire to come to You, but You have said in Your Word, *Him that cometh to me I will in no wise cast out.*"

"Now I know how I come. You have said, *Him that cometh to me I will in no wise cast out.*"

"Now I know how I come. You have said, *Him that cometh to me I will in no wise cast out.*"

"I believe this statement of Yours. Therefore, though I don't feel it, I believe You have received me."

"I believe this statement of Yours. Therefore, though I don't feel it, I believe You have received me.

When he had finished, I said, "Did you really come?"

He replied, "I did."

"Has He received you?"

"I do not feel it," he replied.

"But what does He say?"

"*Him that cometh to me I will in no wise cast out.*"

"Is this true? Does Jesus tell the truth, or does He lie?"

"He tells the truth."

"What, then, must He have done?"

"He must have received me."

"Now," I said, "go to your room; stand firmly on this promise of Jesus Christ. The devil will give you an awful conflict, but just answer him every time with John 6:37, and stand right there, believing what Jesus says in spite of your feelings, in spite of what the devil may say, and in spite of everything."

He went to his room. The devil did give him an awful conflict, but he stood firmly on John 6:37 and came out of his room triumphant and radiant.

Anyone can be saved who will come to Jesus. Years have passed since then. Though the devil has tried again and again to plunge him into despair, he has stood firmly on John 6:37, and he is today being used of God to do larger work for Christ than almost any man I know. He is the author of that hymn:

> Years I spent in vanity and pride,
>   Caring not my Lord was crucified,
> Knowing not it was for me He died
>   On Calvary.

> Mercy there was great, and grace was free,
>   Pardon there was multiplied to me,
> There my burdened soul found liberty,
>   At Calvary.[3]

Lastly, anyone can be saved who will come to Jesus. *The Spirit and the bride say, Come. And he that heareth, let him say, Come. And he that is athirst, let him come: he that will, let him take the water of life freely* (Revelation 22:17). Come now, come.

---

3   William R. Newell, "At Calvary," 1895.

Chapter 10

How to Find Rest

Come unto me, all ye that labor and are heavy
laden, and I will give you rest. Take my yoke upon
you, and learn of me; for I am meek and lowly
in heart: and ye shall find rest unto your souls.
(Matthew 11:28-29)

The night is very dark, but I have a bright text – a good text for a dark night. My subject is what this world needs. You will find it in Matthew 11:28: *Come unto me, all ye that labor and are heavy laden, and I will give you rest.* That is the offer this old world needs. What this world needs is rest. What every man and woman, who has not already found it in Christ, needs is rest. My heart is heavy when I see the millions of people on the earth, the toilers who are working hard for small pay and go home night after night to their wretched homes, all worn out, without any fit place to sleep. But my heart is heavier yet when I see the many more millions who have not only had no rest for the body but also no rest for their heart, no rest for their soul, rich as well as poor.

But I am glad that there is One who can give rest to every tired heart, and that One is Jesus Christ. He stands today with extended hands and says, *Come unto me, all ye that labor and are heavy laden, and I will give you rest.* Now, those are either the words of a divine Being or the words of a lunatic. If the Lord Jesus Christ offers rest and gives it, He is a divine Being; if He offers rest and cannot give it, He is a lunatic. Suppose any man, even the greatest and the best that the world ever saw, should stand and hold out his hands to this sorrowing, grief-stricken, burdened world of ours and say what Jesus said, *Come unto me, and I will give you rest.* You would know at once that the man had gone crazy, for no man could do it. But Jesus offers to do it, and He does it. Thousands, tens of thousands, and millions throughout the centuries have accepted Christ's offer, and nobody ever accepted it yet that did not find rest.

> If the Lord Jesus Christ offers rest and gives it, He is a divine Being; if He offers rest and cannot give it, He is a lunatic.

The Lord Jesus spoke to a great throng that day, perhaps as big as the crowds that gather today, but a more motley crowd. It represented much more misery than this crowd represents. This crowd represents misery enough if we knew everything, but that throng was a more miserable crowd. There were multitudes of the poor near Jesus; the penniless and the sick were there; all kinds of diseases were represented – leprosy, blindness, and every manner of disease. The demoniac, the outcast man and woman, the destitute man and woman, and the degraded man and woman – a vast mass of misery – were all there, and the Lord Jesus Christ cast His loving eye over them. His heart went out to that great multitude that represented so much misery, and He said, "Come, come to Me, every one of you who has a burden, everyone who has a sorrow, everyone who has a broken heart; *come unto me, all ye that labor and are heavy laden, and I will give you rest."*

And do you know, He not only extended His hands to that great throng that represented so much misery, but He also extends His hands to all men and all women in all ages that are burdened, downtrodden, oppressed, wretched, brokenhearted, and despairing? He says to them all, *Come unto me, all ye that labor and are heavy laden, and I will give you rest.* He says the same to you.

All That Labor and Are Heavy Laden

Will you please notice whom it is He has invited – all that labor and are heavy laden. The commentators have tried to tone down the words of our Lord. Some commentators tell us that He meant all who were burdened with the many requirements of the Mosaic law; other commentators tell us He meant all who were burdened by a consciousness of sin, a sense of guilt. But He means just what He says. *Come unto me, all ye that labor –* every man that has a burden, a sorrow, a heartache, a trouble, or a woe of any kind – Jesus invites you to come.

Those Burdened with a Sense of Sin and Shame

First, He invites all of you who are burdened with a sense of sin and a sense of shame. I suppose there are many who have recognized the fact that your life is disgraceful. You are ashamed of yourself. You hardly lift up your head; you dare not lift it up and look your fellow man or woman in the face. You are saying to yourself, "My life is simply shameful," and you are crushed by the sense of your disgrace and your sin. To every one of you Jesus says, "Come unto Me, and I will give you rest."

That day when our Lord Jesus uttered these words in Capernaum, on the outskirts of the crowd was a woman who was a sinner, a professional sinner, an outcast despised by every-one. As she stood on the outskirts of that great crowd, I have no doubt many a woman who prided herself on her own morality turned around and looked at her with scorn. But soon Jesus looked at her too – not with scorn but with pity, compassion, tenderness, yearning, and love. As His eye fell upon her, she looked right at Him and saw that He was speaking directly to her. He seemed to lose sight of everybody else and just stretched His hands out toward her as He uttered the words of the text, *Come unto me, all ye that labor and are heavy laden, and I will give you rest.* That woman said, "He means me," and when the crowd broke up, she followed at a distance to see where Jesus went. Jesus went to the house of Simon, the Pharisee, who had invited Him to dinner.

As soon as she knew where He had gone, she hurried to her home, took out of her treasures a very costly box of oint-ment, the most expensive thing that she had, hurried back to Simon's house, and went through the open door into the open court. As Jesus reclined there in the Oriental way, she went up behind Him, bent over His feet, which were bare in the Oriental fashion, and began to bathe them with her tears. The other guests looked up in scorn. They said, "This man pretends to be a prophet; He is no prophet, or He would not allow that woman to touch Him. If He were a prophet, He would know what kind of a woman she is – that she is a sinner."

Well, He did know. He knew better than any of them knew that she not only was a sinner but that she was also a repent-ing sinner. When His feet were wet with her tears, she took the long tresses of her beautiful hair and wiped His feet with them. Then she broke the alabaster box of precious ointment over them. The Lord Jesus turned to her and said, *Thy sins are forgiven.* Then He said again, *Thy faith hath saved thee; go in peace,* and that woman, who that day stood on the outskirts of that crowd with a broken heart, went away from that house with the rest of God in her heart. Is there any woman like her here, or any man overwhelmed in sin, anyone burdened with a sense of sin and shame? Come to the Lord Jesus Christ, and He will give you rest.

Those Burdened by the Bondage of Sin

In the second place, the Lord Jesus invites every man and woman who is burdened by the bondage of sin. There are men here, for example, who are in bondage to the appetite for strong drink. You want to be sober; you want to lead upright lives; you have tried again and again to give up the drink, but you failed. And this appetite for strong drink is an awful crushing burden. Some of you are burdened with the appetite for morphine or cocaine, or chloral, or heroin.

> Jesus says, "Come unto Me, and I will give you rest."

Oh, how you have tried to be free from your bondage. The Lord Jesus says, "Come unto Me, and I will give you rest."

Some of you are burdened with vileness, with impurity, with disgusting sin. How you hate yourself; how you despise yourself; how you have tried to break away time after time, until at last you have given up. You are utterly discouraged today, crushed by the power of your sin. Jesus says, "Come unto Me, and I will give you rest."

Some of you struggle with some other sin, but if we could read the secret sorrow of your heart, we would find hundreds of men and women crushed to the earth by the power of sin. The Lord Jesus says to every one of you, *Come unto me, all ye that labor and are heavy laden, and I will give you rest.*

I have a very dear friend who was carefully reared by a godly mother. He has as good blood in his veins as there is in America. His mother was afraid that he would become a drunkard, so she begged him to never touch alcoholic liquor.

He lived to eighteen years of age without tasting it. He lived in the country, but one day he went to town with a man. On the way back, the man bought some whiskey and asked him to drink. "No," he said. "I promised my mother never to drink."

"Well," the man said, "if you don't drink, you will insult me." And that elderly man just worked on that boy until he got him to drink his first glass of whiskey. Then the demon in him was set on fire. From that experience, he became almost immediately a drunkard. He went down, down, down in the course of years; he lost one position after another, and in the end he was a wrecked man in New York City. He had written 138 forgeries against his last employer, and the officers of the law were in search of him.

One night, one awful night, he went into a saloon and for a long time sat there in a drunken stupor on a whiskey keg; then, coming out of the stupor, he felt all the horrors of delirium tremens coming over him. He thought he was going to die. He went up to the bar and ordered a glass of whiskey, and he rattled the glass upon the bar so that the bar shook. He said, "Men, hear me, hear me; I shall never drink another glass of whiskey if I die." And they all laughed at him. He went out of the saloon, went to the lockup, and said to the sergeant of police at the desk, "Lock me up; I am going to have the tremens; lock me up."

The sergeant sent him down to the cell and locked him up. He spent a night in awful agony and the next day in awful agony. As the night was coming, somebody said to him, "Why don't you go to Jerry McAuley's Mission?" The lockup was a little way from the McAuley Cremorne Mission. So as best he could, in an awful condition, he went down to Jerry McAuley's Cremorne Mission and listened to one man after another who had been saved, giving their testimonies.

When Jerry McAuley asked all who would receive Christ

to come to the front, he went up to the front, knelt down, and said, "Jerry, pray for me."

Jerry said, "Pray for yourself."

"Oh," he said, "I don't know how to pray. I have forgotten how to pray. Jerry, pray for me."

Jerry said, "Pray for yourself."

That wrecked and ruined man lifted up his broken heart to Jesus. He came to Jesus; Jesus met him immediately and took the appetite for whiskey away from him at once. Today that man is one of the most honored men in New York City.

Some years ago, I was in the city of Washington, and I met the postmaster general of the United States. He asked me if I would go to dinner with him that night after a meeting. I went to dinner at the house of the postmaster general of the United States of America, and as I entered the drawing room, who should I see sitting there as an honored guest but Mr. Samuel Hadley. This poor drunkard of bygone years of whom I have just spoken was an honored guest in the house of the postmaster general of the United States of America.

Are you burdened? Have you fought against sin and failed? Have you tried again and again, perhaps signed pledge after pledge, but only broke them? Have you some other disturbing sin? Are you burdened with the weight of an overcoming sin? Jesus holds out His hand to you. He says, *Come unto me, all ye that labor and are heavy laden, and I will give you rest.*

Those Burdened with Sorrow

He invites everybody burdened with sorrow. If you only knew the sorrows of men and women today. All the light has gone out of the lives of some of you men because your wife has recently died. Some of you sons and daughters are brokenhearted over the recent death of a loving Christian mother. Some of you fathers and mothers are brokenhearted because recently a beloved child has been taken from your home and sleeps in the quiet cemetery. Some of you have met with reverses in business. Some of you have other sorrows, but it doesn't matter what your sorrow is, how peculiar, how great, or how overwhelming. To every sorrowing man and woman, Jesus holds out His hands and says, "Come unto Me and I will give you rest."

Some time ago in our country, there was a gentleman and his wife who had a very happy home. The man was prosperous in business in Cleveland, Ohio, but there came a downturn in business, and the man lost everything he had in the world. The home broke up, and his oldest daughter had to go to work to make a living. His two boys were too young to work. His wife had to leave him and take the two boys to one of the Southern states to the home of a sister where she became a housekeeper to make a living for herself and the boys. The father came to Chicago to see if he could retrieve his fortunes.

> To every sorrowing man and woman, Jesus says, "Come unto Me and I will give you rest."

After his wife had been in the South for some time, hoping that a better day might come again, she received a telegraph saying that her husband was very ill in Chicago, and she had better come at once. She took the train. It was a long journey. She reached Chicago that night and went to the hospital to which her husband had been taken. But by some mistake, the authorities of the hospital said to her, "You cannot see your husband tonight; come at nine o'clock tomorrow morning, and you can see him."

With a heavy heart, she went to a place where she had stopped and then went back to the hospital at nine the next morning. As she rang the bell, they met her at the door and said, "Your husband died last night." She took him out and buried him; her loneliness and sorrow were so great, and her weeping so frequent that it affected her eyesight. She went to a physician.

The physician told her it was not very serious, that she could go back to Mississippi, and her eyes would soon be well. She assumed that he was a regular physician, but she found out afterwards that he was a Christian Science physician who was trying to cure her by making her feel she was not ill. She went back to Mississippi. Her eyes got worse and worse.

She finally went to a regular physician who examined her eyes. He said, "Madam, your case is hopeless. If you had come to me a few weeks ago, I could have helped you. Your problem has become so advanced now that there is absolutely no hope for you. You will be totally blind."

Home broken up, husband buried, eyesight gone. She came to Chicago and dropped in to our church where she heard the gospel. She heard about Jesus and came to Him with all her overwhelming sorrow, and Jesus gave her rest.

And if you come to the prayer meeting at our church on any Friday night, you will see a woman, dressed in black, with a refined, beautiful face, eyes closed, and perfectly sightless, but in that face you will see a more serene and profound joy than you have often seen in a human face. Very likely you will see her rise to her feet in the course of the meeting with a face radiant with the sunshine of heaven; she will tell how wonderfully God has blessed her. You may hear her say what she often says – that she thanks God she lost her sight, for out of her great troubles, she was brought to Christ and found a joy that she never knew before.

There is a place where there is a cure for every sorrow. That place is at the feet of Jesus. I have a beautiful Testament at home that I think very highly of, not because of the beauty of the binding, but because my mother gave it to my grandmother, my father's mother. I think it was at the time of my grandfather's death. On the flyleaf of the Testament in my mother's own beautiful handwriting are these words: "Earth hath no sorrow that heaven cannot heal." That is true, but something better is true. Earth has no sorrow that Jesus cannot heal right now before we get to heaven.

Those Burdened by Doubt and Unbelief

Again, the Lord Jesus invites all who are burdened by doubt and unbelief. To some men doubt and unbelief are not a burden. They are glad that they are skeptics. They are proud of their doubts. But to an earnest-minded man, to a man of any real moral earnestness, doubt is a burden, a heavy load; he is never proud of doubt. He never rejoices in doubt. An earnest-minded man doesn't want doubt but truth; not uncertainty, but certainty; not agnosticism, but knowledge of God.

I don't doubt that in this great crowd some people honestly doubt, and your doubt is a burden. Well, Jesus says to you, "Come unto Me, all ye that are burdened with doubt, and I will give you rest."

"What!" you say. "A skeptic come to Christ, an unbeliever come to Christ, an agnostic come to Christ?"

Certainly! He is the best One you can come to. Thomas was a skeptic. The other disciples had seen our Lord after His resurrection, but Thomas was not present. When Thomas came back, the other disciples said, *We have seen the Lord.*

He said, "I don't believe a word of it. I don't believe you have seen the Lord, and I won't believe it unless I see with my own eyes and put my fingers into the prints of the nails in His hand and thrust my hand into His side." But Thomas was an honest doubter, and when he thought that the Lord Jesus might be around the next Sunday evening, he was there. He came to Jesus with his doubts. Jesus scattered every one of them, and Thomas cried, *My Lord and my God.*

Nathaniel was a doubter, an honest doubter, a thoroughgoing skeptic. Philip came to him and said, "Nathaniel, *we have found him, of whom Moses in the law, and the prophets, wrote, Jesus of Nazareth, the son of Joseph."*

Nathaniel said, "I don't believe He is the Messiah. He came from Nazareth, then He is not the Messiah. *Can any good thing come out of Nazareth?"*

Philip said, *"Come and see."* Ah, that is the thing to do; come and see.

Nathaniel said, "I will come." He went with Philip; he met the Lord, and he had not been with the Lord ten minutes before all his doubts were gone. Nathaniel cried, *Thou art the Son of God; thou art King of Israel* (John 1:45-49).

If you are burdened with doubt, bring your doubts to Jesus. Whatever your burden is, Jesus invites you, every burdened one, every heavyhearted one, to come unto Him. "Come unto Me, and I will give you rest."

Will you please notice what Jesus invites you to do? Jesus says, *Come unto me* – not come unto the church; the church cannot give you rest. I believe in the church; I believe every converted man ought to be a member of some church, but the church never gave anybody rest. The church is full of people today who have never found rest. They have come to the church instead of coming to Jesus Himself.

Jesus does not say, "Come to a creed." I believe in creeds. I think every man ought to have a creed. A creed is simply an intelligent, systematic statement of what a man believes, and a man ought to believe something and ought to be able to state intelligently what he believes. If he is an intelligent, studious man, his creed will be getting longer all the time. I have a creed, a great, long one. It is getting longer every day, for I am learning something new every day, but no creed ever gave anybody rest. Consider the *Thirty-nine Articles;* they won't give you rest. Consider the *Westminster Catechism;* it is a good creed, but it won't give you rest. There was never a creed written or printed that would give anybody rest. Rest comes from the personal Savior. Many men are orthodox, orthodox enough for anybody with a great, long creed, but they never came to the personal Jesus and never found rest.

The Lord Jesus does not say, "Come unto the pope," or "Come unto the priest," or "Come unto the preacher," or "Come unto the evangelist," or "Come unto any other man." He says, *Come unto me.* No preacher can give you rest; no priest can give you rest; no pope can give you rest; no man can give you rest. Jesus says, *Come unto me.*

I have sometimes asked people if they have come to Jesus, and they say, "Oh, I am a Protestant." Well, that never saved anybody. There will be many Protestants in hell.

Others say, "I am a Roman Catholic." That never saved anybody either. There will be many Roman Catholics in hell.

When a man says, "I am a Roman Catholic," I say, "I am not asking you that. Have you come to Jesus?" It is not a question of whether you are a Roman Catholic or a Protestant. Have you come to Jesus? If you have not, will you come now?

Men are so anxious to put somebody else in the place of Jesus – to come to some man. A lady said to me one night in my own church, "I am a Roman Catholic. I like to come to hear you preach, and I would like to ask you a question. Can I come and confess to you? I want to confess to somebody."

Jesus can and He will give rest to anyone who comes to Him.

"No, you can't," I said. "You need to come to Jesus."

Come unto me, says Jesus. Nobody but Jesus can give you rest. Jesus can and He will give rest to anyone who comes to Him. *Come unto me, all ye that labor and are heavy laden, and I will give you rest. Take my yoke upon you, and learn of me; for I am meek and lowly in heart: and ye shall find rest unto your souls. For my yoke is easy, and my burden is light* (Matthew 11:28-30).

Come to Jesus, take His yoke, surrender absolutely to Him; commit all your sins to Him to pardon; commit all your doubts to Him to remove; commit all your thoughts to Him to teach; commit yourself to Him to believe in Him, to learn from Him, to obey Him, and to serve Him. The moment you come to Him with all your heart and cast yourself upon Him, He will give you rest. You can have rest right now; right there sitting in your chair this moment, you can have rest. Jesus is nearer to you than the man in the next seat. Say, "Jesus, I come," and He will give you rest.

One night in my church in Chicago, one of the officers of my church went around the upper gallery after I was through preaching. As the people were going out, this officer stepped up to a gentleman and said, "Are you saved?"

"Yes, sir," he said, "I am saved." He was very positive about it.

"How long have you been saved?"

He said, "About five minutes."

"When were you saved?"

"About five minutes ago, while that man was preaching."

He did not wait until I got through my sermon. He came to Jesus right then, and Jesus saved him at that moment.

Will you come? Don't look at me. Don't look at Mr. Alexander. Look to the Lord Jesus standing there, holding out His hands to you with a heart bursting with love, breaking with pity and compassion, and saying to every heavyhearted man and woman, *Come unto me, all ye that labor and are heavy laden, and I will give you rest.* Will you come?

Chapter 11

Joy Unspeakable and Full of Glory

Though now ye see him not, yet believing, ye rejoice greatly with joy unspeakable and full of glory. (1 Peter 1:8)

Christians are the happiest people in the world. According to our text, they *rejoice greatly with joy unspeakable and full of glory,* and nobody else does. I will tell you why Christians are happy.

Their Sins Are Forgiven

First, real Christians are happy because they know that their sins are forgiven. Nobody in this world knows that his sins are forgiven except a Christian. If any man or woman who is not a Christian says, "I know my sins are forgiven," they say what is not true, for their sins are not forgiven. But every true Christian knows that his sins are forgiven – all forgiven.

You say, "How do they know that?"

Because God says so. If you will turn to Acts 13:39, you will see that *every one that believeth is justified from all things.* God says so. A woman who had been a sinner came to Christ one day. She washed His feet with her tears and wiped them with the hair of her head. Men looked on in scorn, but Jesus turned to her and said, "Woman, thy sins, which are many, are all forgiven" (Luke 7:47), and she went out of that place knowing that her sins were all forgiven. She knew it because Jesus said so.

And God says just as distinctly in the verse I have just quoted that every Christian's sins are forgiven, just as Jesus said it to the woman. Christians know their sins are forgiven in a second way – because the Holy Spirit bears witness in their hearts that their sins are forgiven. One day the apostle Peter was preaching in the household of Cornelius and speaking about Jesus. He said, *To him bear all the prophets witness, that through his name every one that believeth on him shall receive remission of sins* (Acts 10:43). Cornelius and his whole household believed it, and immediately the Spirit of God came upon them.

> There is no joy on earth like the joy of knowing that God has forgiven and blotted out every sin you ever committed.

When you and I believe in Jesus, His Spirit comes into our hearts and bears witness with our spirit that our sins are all forgiven and that we are children of God. There is no joy on earth like the joy of knowing that God has forgiven and blotted out every sin you ever committed.

Suppose a person was in prison for life for some crime, and someone brought him a pardon; don't you think he would be happy? The governor of the state of Pennsylvania once decided to pardon a man, and he sent Mr. Moody to tell him that he was pardoned. Mr. Moody went to the prison. He was going to preach a sermon, but before he began the sermon he said, "The governor of the state has handed me a pardon for one of you."

He was not going to tell who the man was until he got through the sermon. But as he looked over the crowd of men, he saw there was such suspense and such agony, every one of them wondering whether he was the one, that he said, "This will never do, to keep these men in suspense. I must tell them at once who the man is." So he said, "The man who is pardoned is . . . ." And oh, the joy that filled that man's heart when he knew that out of that great company of criminals, he was the one whom the governor had pardoned.

But it is nothing to know that one is pardoned here on earth compared to knowing that God has forgiven all your sins and blotted them out. Oh, the joy that comes into the heart when a man knows that every sin he ever committed is pardoned and blotted out, and that God has absolutely nothing against him.

A great king once wrote a song that has lived through the centuries. It was a song of joy. That great king had been a great sinner, and God had forgiven his sin. He had much to make a man happy, and he was the greatest king of his day. He had great wealth; he had great armies; he was the greatest general of the time; and he had a great palace. But when he came to write his song of joy, he did not say, "Happy is the man that has a beautiful palace"; he did not say, "Happy is the man that has great armies"; he did not say, "Happy is the man that is a great general"; he did not say, "Happy is the man that is beloved by his people." He said, "Oh, *blessed is he whose transgression is forgiven, whose sin is covered. Blessed is the man unto whom Jehovah imputeth not iniquity, and in whose spirit there is no guile*" (Psalm 32:1-2). Every man who takes the Lord Jesus as his Savior will have his sins all forgiven and will have the joy of knowing that every sin is blotted out.

Freed from Sin's Power

In the second place, Christians are happy because they are set free from sin's power. Now, everybody that sins is a slave. They are slaves to sin. Years ago, when I was a boy in the Southern states, where Mr. Alexander comes from, there were slaves. The black men were slaves. Some of the masters were kind, and some of the masters were cruel – so very, very cruel; it makes one's heart ache to think what those poor black men suffered!

But there was never a slave owner in the South that was as cruel a master as Satan, and there was never a bondage as awful as the bondage of sin. Some women are bound by the appetite for strong drink. I presume some of you men have also tried to break away from alcohol, but you are enslaved by it. Some of you are enslaved by morphine, some by heroin, some by cocaine, some by a bad temper, some by an ungovernable tongue, and some by other things, but every man or woman without Christ is a slave.

But when you come to Jesus Christ, He sets you free. He says in John 8:31-32, *If ye abide in my word, then are ye truly my disciples; and ye shall know the truth, and the truth shall make you free.* In verse 36 He says, *If therefore the Son shall make you free, ye shall be free indeed.* The Lord Jesus Christ takes every man and every woman that believes in Him and sets them free from the power of sin, strong drink, heroin, a bad temper, impurity, profanity – from the power of every sin.

I was reading the life story of a very dear friend of mine. I have read it a number of times before, but I read it again this morning. He told how one night, after he had been a slave for years, he knelt down and prayed at a mission, and Jesus Christ met him and set him free. And he said, "From that day until this, I have never had the least desire for strong drink." When he went out of that mission that night, he knew that after years of slavery and ruin, he was a free man. He just shouted for joy,

"Glory to God," and he has been shouting ever since. I wish he were here today so you might hear him shout. I wish he were here on this platform so you could look into his face. Oh, the joy of being set free from sin after days and weeks or months or maybe years of slavery.

Children of God

In the third place, Christians are happy because they know that they are children of God. It is a wonderful thing to know that you are a child of God. No one knows it but the Christian, for no one is a child of God but the Christian. You say, "How does the Christian know that he is a child of God?" Because God says so. In John 1:12, He says that *as many as received him, to them gave he the right to become children of God, even to them that believe on his name.* If any man or woman, young or old, receives the Lord Jesus Christ, you will be a child of God that very moment and will know that you are a child of God.

Isn't that enough to be happy over? Suppose you knew that you were the son of some great man, or the son of a millionaire, or the son of a king, or the son of an emperor; don't you think you would be happy? But it is nothing to be the son of any king or any emperor compared to being the son of God, the King of Kings.

One day years ago, an English duke lay dying. He called his younger brother, the one next in line to him, to his bedside and said, "Brother, in a few hours you will be a duke – and I will be a king." He was a Christian; he was a child of a king, and he knew that when he left his dukedom down here, he would get a kingdom up there.

I say to the poorest man or woman this afternoon, young or old, if you will receive Jesus Christ, the moment you do so, you can lift your head and say, "I am a child of the King; I know I am a child of God."

Sometimes, as I travel around the world, people will point out a man to me and say, "That man is the son of such and such a great man." Pointing one out to me in Germany, they said, "That is the son of such and such a king"; in another place they said, "That is the son of such and such a king." What of it? Suppose he is a child of a king; I am a child of God. That is better than being a child of a king.

> **A true Christian that believes the Bible, studies it, and remembers it, is not afraid of anything or anybody.**

Now, it has been suggested that you put silver in the collection plate. Well, I guess that some of you cannot put silver in, but I want to say that if you can only put copper in it, you are just as welcome as anybody, and if you can't put copper in, you are still just as welcome as anybody.

We read in the Bible that unto the poor, the gospel was preached. I believe in preaching to the rich; they need it as much as anybody. But, thank God, the woman who had to walk here because she didn't have money enough to pay a penny for the bus, the poorest woman, or the richest can become a child of God in a moment by taking Jesus Christ. I would rather be the poorest woman that is a child of God than the richest woman that is a child of the devil.

Delivered from All Fear

Again, Christians are happy because they are delivered from all fear. A true Christian that believes the Bible, studies it, and remembers it is not afraid of anything or anybody. Now a great many people who are very rich have all their joy spoiled because they are constantly thinking that some calamity may overtake them. Rich men don't enjoy their riches because they are afraid of losing them, and people who have their friends around them don't enjoy their friends because they are afraid they will die. People who have all the comforts of life don't enjoy them because they fear that some calamity may come and sweep the comforts away. Those with very little, who are barely making a living, don't enjoy it because they fear they may be thrown out of work and not be able to make a living. But the true Christian is delivered from all that fear. There is one verse in the Bible which, if you are a child of God and believe it and keep it in mind, will take away all anxiety as long as you live. That is Romans 8:28: *And we know that to them that love God all things work together for good.*

Sometimes the devil whispers to me, "Perhaps you will lose everything you have in the world."

"Well," I say, "it doesn't make any difference if I do. If I do, that will be one of the *all things,* and *all things work together for good."*

Sometimes when I am away from my family, the devil whispers to me, "Your wife is ill," or "Your son is ill," or "Your daughters are ill and will die before you ever see them again."

I don't know how often the devil has come and whispered that. When he does, I just lift my head and say, "Well, that cannot be unless it is the will of God, my Father. And if they do die, it is one of the *all things [that] work together for good."*

The devil comes sometimes and whispers, "Perhaps you will be taken ill; perhaps you will lose your eyesight or your hearing and not be able to preach anymore."

I just lift my head and say, "Well, if I do, it will be one of the *all things,* and *to them that love God all things work together for good."* So you see, if a person is a real Christian and believes the Bible and bears it in mind, he is not afraid of calamity, neither is he afraid of any man.

So many people are afraid of men and are tormented by

the fear of men. Many of you today would profess to being Christians, but you are afraid some man or woman might see you; you are afraid that you will be laughed at and that you will be persecuted in the mill, or the factory, or the shop. But a Christian is not afraid of man. The Christian reads Romans 8:31 and says, *If God is for us, who is against us?* A Christian does not fear the face of any man or woman on earth.

One time in Chicago a man came to me and said, "You had better look out; there is a man who says he has it in for you." He told me who the man was – a very desperate man, a man willing to do almost anything.

Well, I was not troubled a bit. I did not lie awake a single night; I was not troubled for two seconds. I said, "That's all right. I know he is quite powerful, and I have reason to believe he is unprincipled, but I know that I am right with God; God is on my side, and if God has agreed to take care of me, that man can't touch me, unless it is God's will." A living faith in Jesus Christ takes all fear of man away forever.

It takes away the fear of death. I know many people whose lives are shadowed and darkened by the fear of death. Right in the midst of health and strength, they say, "Oh, what if I should be taken with tuberculosis or get heart disease, diphtheria, smallpox, or some other terrible disease?" But a Christian is not afraid of death. Death has lost all its terrors for the Christian. A Christian knows that death for him is simply to depart and be with Christ.

One evening in Chicago, I went to see a young lady who had sung in my choir – a very beautiful, attractive girl whose life had been full of promise, but she had been suddenly afflicted with rapid tuberculosis. She had probably only a few days to live. As it turned out, she did not have a day to live. I was told that she would like to see me, so I went. I entered the room where the young girl, cut down in the very blossom of young womanhood, was lying upon her bed. I sat down by her deathbed, and her face shone like an angel's. I said, "Humanly speaking, there is no hope for your recovery."

She said, "I know; I don't care to recover. I would have been glad to recover to serve Christ if it had been His will, but since He has decided I can't recover and must very soon leave this world, I wanted to see you and tell you that I don't fear death. I am looking forward to what men call death with great joy and with great anticipation." I went to my church to preach, and when I got up to the pulpit, they brought me a note. That dying girl had asked for paper, and she wrote a note and sent it over to the choir of the church. She told them how happy she was as she lay face-to-face with death and eternity. I tell you it is a joyful thing to have no fear of death.

A Christian is delivered from fear of eternity. But to people without Christ, eternity is a dreadful thing to think about; for people in Christ, eternity is about the sweetest thing there is to think about.

> For people in Christ, eternity is about the sweetest thing there is to think about.

One word fills the heart of the Christian with joy, but fills the heart of the unsaved with terror. That word is *eternity.* I love that word *eternity,* where all sorrow is over forever – all separation, all sickness, all death – where all is eternal sunshine. How I love that word *eternity.*

But some of you don't love it. I have received letters from people who say they wish that I would not talk so much about eternity. I heard of one man who did not want to come to the meetings because I talked too much about eternity. But Christians like to have me talk of eternity.

Write out a card with these words: *Where will you spend eternity?* Hand it to a man who is not a Christian, and it will make him mad. Hand it to a Christian, and it will make him glad. He will answer, "Why, I will spend eternity with Christ in glory."

Assurance of Eternal Life

That leads me to the next reason why Christians are happy. It is because they know that they will live forever. It is a wonderful thing to know that you will never die, that throughout the endless ages of God, you will live on and on and on. As we read in 1 John 2:17: *And the world passeth away, and the lust thereof: but he that doeth the will of God abideth for ever.* And we read in John 3:36: *He that believeth on the Son hath eternal life; but he that believeth not the Son shall not see life, but the wrath of God abideth on him.*

Before I was a Christian, I did not like to look into the future, but how I love to look into the future now. Very often I sit in my room and say, "I wonder how many years I will have to preach." Well, I can't have very many more at the most, probably about twenty, possibly twenty-five, barely possibly thirty years. That is not very much; and then what? Eternity! That is better than preaching. It is a great joy to preach, but oh, to be able to stand and look down through the coming ages and see them roll on, age upon age and age upon age, and know that you are going to live for all eternity in happiness and joy ever increasing! I don't wonder that Christians are happy. I don't wonder that they have *joy unspeakable and full of glory.*

Inheritance

Two other reasons Christians are happy: one is because they know that they are heirs, heirs of God and joint heirs with Jesus Christ. They know that they have *an inheritance incorruptible, and undefiled, and that fadeth not away, reserved in heaven for [them]* (1 Peter 1:4). When one rides down your beautiful English country roads and looks out on the beautiful mansions and manor houses and sees the lakes, forests, parks, and the gardens, one says, "It must be very pleasant to live in there."

Well, I suppose it is, but how long will they live there? The father of the family will probably live ten years, twenty perhaps; the children will live forty or fifty, possibly sixty. Soon gone, soon gone. But every man, woman, and child who receives Jesus will have an inheritance that will last forever, *an inheritance incorruptible, and undefiled, and that fadeth not away.* Every earthly inheritance soon fails; even the richest man on earth won't keep his property very long. But the poorest man or woman today, young or old, who will receive Jesus Christ, will get an inheritance that will last forever.

One day a poor English girl rode along in a third-class carriage; she was very plainly dressed as she looked out the window. They passed by beautiful farms, beautiful trees, beautiful mansions, and every little while a person who sat near the poor girl heard her say, "That belongs to my Father." They would come to a farm, and she would say, "That belongs to my Father"; then to a beautiful mansion, and she would say, "That belongs to my Father too." Then they would pass a lordly castle, and she would say, "That belongs to my Father."

Finally, the man who was listening turned to her and said, "Well, miss, you must have a rich father, for you have been saying for miles as we passed along, 'That belongs to my Father.' Your father must own a great deal of property. He must be a very rich man."

She said, "He is – I am a child of God." She was very rich.

Some of you are having a hard time in this world. I suppose you have to work long hours for small pay. Your homes are not very comfortable. Well, I want to tell you that you won't have to live in them very long. If you will take Christ, you are going to such a mansion as this earth never saw, to such an inheritance as no man ever inherited on this earth. When you go past the rich man's mansion, you say, "I wish I had a home like that." You would not keep it for long. If you will receive Jesus Christ, you will know that you are an heir to all God has. The whole world belongs to Him – the cattle on a thousand hills. If you are a child of God, if you will receive Christ, you will be an heir to all He is and all He has. You can become an heir today.

Indwelling Holy Spirit

One more reason Christians are happy is that God gives Christians the Holy Spirit to dwell in their hearts, and when the Holy Spirit dwells in the heart, He fills the heart with sunshine and gladness, and joy unspeakable. One Monday morning a poor woman came to my door, rang the bell, and said she wanted to see me. The girl who assists me said, "You know he sees no one on Mondays."

She said, "I know it, but I have got to see him."

So the girl called me down, and when I came down, I saw one of the members of my church – a poor washerwoman who had to work hard for her living. "Oh," she said, "Mr. Torrey, I knew you didn't see anybody on Mondays, and I don't like to trouble you, but I received the Holy Spirit last night. I could not sleep all night, and I made up my mind that I was going to give up one day's work and just come around and tell you how happy I was. I just had to. I can't very well afford to give up a day's work, but my heart is so full of joy I could not keep still. I had to tell somebody, and I didn't know anybody else I wanted to tell as much as I wanted to tell you. Though I knew you didn't see anybody on Mondays, I thought you would be glad to have me come and tell you."

"Yes," I said, "I am glad."

That woman was so happy that she could not work; her heart was full of joy.

So, I don't care how dark your heart is today, or how full of sadness it is. I don't care how full of bitterness you are or how hopeless you feel. If you will receive Jesus Christ as your Savior and surrender your whole heart and your whole life to Him as your Lord and Master, there will come into your heart sweetness beyond anything to be known this side of heaven.

Christians rejoice with *joy unspeakable and full of glory.* But you have to be real Christians. Just going to church won't do it, and just saying your prayers won't do it. Just reading your catechism won't do it, and just reading the Bible won't do it. Reading the prayer book, being baptized, being confirmed, or going to the Lord's Supper won't do it. But if you will take Jesus into your heart to be your Savior to rule and reign there and surrender all to Him, I will guarantee that every one of you will get a joy that is heaven begun below.

People say to me, "Do you expect to go to heaven?" Yes, I know I am going to heaven, but thank God, I am in heaven now. I live in a present heaven as I am on my way to the future heaven. I feel like singing all the time. I used to be one of the most melancholy men on earth. I was constitutionally melancholy. I was despondent; I was gloomy. I inherited it from both sides. I used to sit and have the blues by the hour. But do you know, I never have had the blues since I really took the Lord Jesus. I have had trouble; I have had losses; I have seen everything I had in the world swept away, so that I had nothing left. I have seen the time when I had a wife and four children and not a penny to buy them the next meal with. But it came in time, for I knew where to go – straight to God. I have seen times when I didn't have the rent for the house or the wood for the fire in a bitter, cold winter. But I was happy.

I have been in a foreign country where I could not talk the language, and somehow or other there was a failure of supplies.

> But if you will take Jesus into your heart I will guarantee that every one of you will get a joy that is heaven begun below.

I was penniless in a foreign city with a wife and child, hardly knowing anybody in the whole place. But I was happy. I knew whom I trusted. I knew He would get me out somehow, and He did. If you want darkness turned into sunshine, if you want sadness turned into joy, if you want despair turned into glory, if you want defeat turned into victory, if you want all that is bad turned into all that is good – take the Lord Jesus Christ, and take Him right now.

Chapter 12

The Fear of Man Bringeth a Snare

The fear of man bringeth a snare; but whoso putteth his trust in Jehovah shall be safe. (Proverbs 29:25)

Two ways exist – one of ruin, the other of salvation. *The fear of man bringeth a snare* – ruin! *But whoso putteth his trust in Jehovah shall be safe* – the way of salvation; trust in the Lord. Even if you do not believe another verse in the Bible, you know that verse is true. I don't care how much of an infidel any man may be, he knows that the fear of man brings a snare.

Ensnared by the Fear of Man

Many people have been snared by the fear of man. Many a young woman has come to the city from a country village as an innocent, guileless, pure, upright girl, but loving merriment. Coming to the city, she has sought amusement where a poor girl is likely to seek it – in the theater or the dance hall, but intending no wrong. And one night as she returns from a dance with a young man in whom she has become interested and who has been kind to her, he makes advances that the modesty of the girl resents. She blushes. She is indignant.

He laughs at her. "Oh," he says, "you don't understand. I don't mean anything wrong. Everyone does this in the city. You know city life is freer than country life. You don't understand – that's all." He laughs at the girl, and she permits what she at first resented.

A few nights later he goes a little further. Again she is indignant, and again he laughs at her and laughs her out of her puritanical scruples as he calls them. Then he goes further, and soon that girl is on the street ruined, dishonored, belonging to the most wretched class that lives – an outcast woman. The fear of man, the fear of someone's ridicule, has brought a snare that has landed that girl in the slums.

Many a young man has come to the city. He knew enough about life to know that any use of intoxicating liquor is dangerous in the day in which you and I live. His father and mother brought him up with habits of self-restraint and total abstinence, and he is resolved that in coming to the city he will never visit a saloon, that he will never drink even a glass of beer or wine. But one night he is out with his new friends for some entertainment. After the entertainment is over, they propose going to a tavern for just one glass of beer.

"No," he says, "I never drink; it is perilous to drink. I was brought up as a total abstainer, and I intend to remain a total abstainer until the day of my death."

They laugh at him. "Oh," they say, "be a man. Nobody but mamas' boys are total abstainers. If you are going to amount to anything in the city, you must take an occasional glass of beer. Of course, we don't want you to go to excess. We don't believe in overindulgence, but one glass of beer won't hurt you. Come, be a man."

He takes his first glass of beer. It rouses the demon that is in him. That leads to another and another and many others, and now that young fellow is a bloated, ruined, penniless drunkard on the streets of the city. The fear of man has brought a snare that has ruined him for time and eternity.

A few weeks ago, I received one of the saddest letters I ever received from a friend. It was a letter from his brother's wife. This brother of my friend was a very brilliant man, a man of the greatest promise, extraordinary promise, but he started drinking. He found that the drink was controlling him, so he quit and became a total abstainer. He had an opportunity to go to London to visit one of the best-known men, a man that all Englishmen know by name. That man had potential to promote him to great honor. When he went for a visit, this man offered him a glass of wine at his table.

He didn't dare offend his powerful friend by refusing the glass of wine. He thought, "It is only one glass." He took it. He was mad. He rushed from that house, went to a tavern, and then to another, and for days his friends did not know where he was. They sent detectives on his track, who found him helplessly drunk in one of the lowest dens in London, and he has been drinking from that day to this. The brokenhearted wife wrote my friend, his brother, and said, "He is crazy. He has gone and ruined his family; his home is broken; all our prospects are marred; he is lost; he is mad." The fear of man brought a snare.

Many a young fellow has come to the city, thinking he was too much of a man to gamble, for no man who gambles is much of a man. He thinks he is too much of a man to gamble, but he likes an occasional innocent game of cards. One night he is playing cards with his friends, and someone suggests that they just put up a three-penny bid to make it interesting. That is all.

"Oh," they say, "we don't care for the money, but it is just to lend interest to the game."

"No," he says, "I never gamble. I think gambling is stealing."

He is right, for gambling is stealing. No self-respecting man will gamble, for no self-respecting man wants another man's money. I don't see how a man who has taken another man's money by gambling can look in the mirror. I should think he would be ashamed to look himself in the face.

He says, "No, gambling is outright dishonesty; I never gamble."

"Oh," they say, "it is not gambling; it is just for a little amusement. You'd better go home and go to Sunday school. Go and sit with your mother." And they laugh him into his first game of cards.

The gambler's passion – a harder passion to overcome than the appetite for drink ever was – seizes him, and today he is behind prison bars, because he gambled until he took his employer's money to gamble with. The fear of man had brought a snare that has landed him in prison.

Ensnared into a Denial of the Lord

Again, the fear of man ensnares Christians into a denial of their Lord. It snared Peter. Thank God, the time came when Peter threw his fear to the wind and stood before the very men who condemned Jesus to die; he confessed his Lord and rebuked their sin. But that night, after he had told his Lord that though all forsake Him, he never would, he stood before the servant girl who accused him of being a follower of Jesus of Nazareth and said, "I don't know the man." Then a few moments after, he repeated his denial, and an hour later, with oaths and cursings, frightened by what a servant girl might do or say, he denied his Lord again.

Many of you are doing the same thing every day. Down in your office, or your shop, or your factory, or your mill, Jesus Christ is ridiculed. Hard things are said about the Bible; the name of the Lord who died on the cross of Calvary for you is blasphemed; and you are not man enough, you are not woman enough, to stand up and say, "I am a Christian. I believe in that Christ whom you are ridiculing. I believe in that Bible you are laughing at." You are afraid to be laughed at, and the fear of man ensnares you into a denial of the Lord who died on the cross for you.

Ensnared into Compromise

Again, the fear of man ensnares professing Christians into a guilty compromise with the world. Many of you professing Christians are doing things in family life, in social life, and in business life that you know are wrong. Your best moral judgment condemns you for them every time you do them, but you say, "Well, everybody does it. I will be considered odd if I don't. I will be ostracized from my group."

A Christian man, living in one of the suburbs of Chicago where there is a great deal of the form of godliness but very little of the real power, said to me, "My daughter is practically shunned in this suburb because she won't dance, play cards, or go to the theater." Thank God, she was woman enough, young girl though she was, to be willing to be excluded rather than compromise. Many of you are not. You would rather not go to the theater, but you go, even though you don't feel happy there. You would rather not play cards. You know the peril of it. You know how many family card parties have been the door through which a son has become a gambler. You would rather not dance. Your better self is shocked, as the modesty of every intelligent thinking woman must be shocked, at what you see in every ballroom: a familiarity of contact permitted between

> **You are afraid to be laughed at, and the fear of man ensnares you into a denial of the Lord.**

the sexes that is nowhere else permitted in decent society. You know it. You are shocked by it. You don't enjoy it, but you are not brave enough to stand for modesty, purity, and God. The fear of man has entangled you in a snare which has robbed you by your compromise of every bit of real power for Jesus Christ.

Ensnared into Silence and Inactivity

Again, the fear of man ensnares Christians into a guilty silence and inactivity. Many of you attend every meeting, and when the invitation is given for Christians to go speak to the unsaved, you want to do it. You would like to help someone to Christ. What a joy it would be to you, but you say, "Suppose I talk to somebody, and they don't like it. Suppose they laugh at me; suppose they say some hard things to me." The fear of man in and outside these meetings, in your home, in your shop, or in your hotel is shutting your mouth and robbing you of the transcendent joy of leading others to Jesus Christ.

Well, suppose they do laugh at you. Remember that they spit in your Master's face. They won't spit in yours. They struck Him with their fists. They probably won't strike you. They nailed Him to the cross. Aren't you willing to be laughed at for a Master like that? I believe that the fear of man on the part of professing Christians is keeping them back from giving their testimony for Christ and working to bring others to Christ. That is doing far more to hinder the work of God than any other cause today. Men are being saved by the thousands, but if you Christians would throw your fear to the wind on the streets, in the shops, in the homes, and in the hotels, you would have the boldness to witness and work for your Master, and they would be saved by the tens of thousands.

Ensnared into Rejection

Again, the fear of man ensnares those who are not Christians into the rejection of Jesus Christ. Hundreds of men and women would like to be Christians. They see the joy of it. They see that the Christian life is beyond a doubt the better life for the present as well as for the future, but they are afraid that if they accept Christ, somebody will ridicule them. The fear of man is shutting them out of the acceptance of Jesus Christ. I believe that more people are kept from accepting Christ every day by the fear of what someone will say or do than by any other cause. If we could get rid of this fear, I believe there would be five hundred or a thousand saved every day instead of two hundred or three hundred.

Ensnared into Discouraging Public Confession

Also, the fear of man ensnares those who really think they have accepted Christ into not making a public confession of Him. Now Jesus says distinctly: *Every one therefore who shall confess me before men, him will I also confess before my Father who is in heaven. But whosoever shall deny me before men, him will I also deny before my Father who is in heaven* (Matthew 10:32-33). Paul says distinctly: *With the heart man believeth unto righteousness; and with the mouth confession is made unto salvation* (Romans 10:10). And yet a host of you are trying to be Christians and never stand up to say so. You don't admit that it is the fear of man that keeps you from doing it.

"Oh no," you say, "I don't believe in this publicity. I don't believe in this standing-up business. I believe in doing things more quietly. I don't believe in excitement." You give a thousand and one reasons, but men, if you were honest with yourselves, as you will have to be honest with God someday, and told the truth, you would say, "It is because I am afraid to do it."

When we were in Edinburgh, a fine-looking young fellow came to me one day and said, "I am a coward."

I said, "What is the matter?"

He said, "I thought I accepted Christ here the other night, and I have not been man enough to tell another man in the office what I have done. I am a coward."

Well, he was. So are you. You professed to take Jesus Christ. You quietly told somebody, but to this day you have not told the other men in your office, in your home, in your hotel, or in your shop. The fear of man has sealed your mouth, made you a blatant coward, and robbed you of all the joy that there is in a complete Christian experience.

Ensnared into Discouragement

The fear of man ensnares those who begin the Christian life from continuing in it, because somebody says some discouraging thing. One night, when we were in a Scottish town, two young men both professed to accept Christ. The pastor of one of them sat on the platform. He went to his pastor and told him what he had done, and his pastor encouraged him. The other man's pastor was one of these fun-loving pastors, a man whose chief function is to serve as a figurehead at big feasts and encourage the fast men of the town by drinking their wine and joining in their tastes. If there is any man on earth for whom I am tempted to have utter contempt, it is a fun-loving minister, the minister whose chief function is to adorn big suppers and drink rich men's wines. I would rather be an outright pub owner or an alcohol seller any day than a preacher of that kind. I have more respect for a good, straight-out alcohol seller than that kind of a preacher.

This man was that kind of a preacher. He had occasionally been seen on the streets when he needed the whole sidewalk. The young man went to his preacher and told him what he had done. His preacher said, "Don't you believe a word they are saying up there." He discouraged the young man. If there is a deeper spot in hell than any other, it is for the man that bears the name of minister and dares to discourage the young convert in his first aspirations toward God. Well, this man did, and the poor young fellow was discouraged quite entirely. Not excusable, but a minister of the gospel had laughed at him and snared him into wretched backsliding and maybe into hell. If you are starting out in the Christian life, no matter who approves or disapproves, you are right. Go on in spite of everybody.

> If you are starting out in the Christian life, no matter who approves or disapproves, you are right.

Ensnared into Eternal Ruin

The fear of man ensnares people into their eternal ruin. Many men and women lie in Christless graves today and will pass to a Christless eternity, because the fear of man kept them from the acceptance of Christ. When I am home in Chicago, if I have a night off, I often run out to another city to help ministers. One night I crossed the state line about twenty miles from Chicago into the city of Hammond, Indiana. After speaking, I gave the invitation, and among those who were moved by the Spirit of God was a young woman. She rose to her feet and started to come to the front. The young man who sat beside her touched her arm. He was engaged to marry her. He said, "Don't go tonight. If you will wait for a few days, I may go with you."

For fear of offending her fiancé, she sat down. I went back the next week to speak in the opera house. At the close of the meeting, two young women came and said, "Oh, Mr. Torrey, as soon as you can get away from the opera house, come with us. A young lady was going to come forward the other night, but the young man to whom she is engaged asked her to wait. She did wait, and now she has erysipelas.[4] It has gone to her brain, and she is dying. She probably won't live until morning. Come to see her as soon as you can."

I hurried along from the opera house. I entered her home, went into the room where the poor girl lay dying, her face all painted black with iodine. She was hardly recognizable as the same person, but was perfectly conscious. I urged her then to receive Christ immediately. "No," she said. "I was about to the last time you were here, but I didn't do it then. I am dying; I can't do it now."

I pleaded with her. I begged her. I knew it was her last hour. I did everything, but she would not yield, and when I passed out of that room of awful darkness, a young man in the hallway grasped me by the hand, took me into a cold dark room, and though I could not see him, I could feel he was shaking like a leaf. "Oh," he said, "Mr. Torrey, I am engaged to marry that girl. When you spoke here last week, we were both at the meeting. When you gave the invitation, she started for the front. I said, 'No, don't go; if you wait for me a few days, I may go with you.' She didn't go, and now she is dying without Christ. She is lost, and I am to blame. I am to blame."

The Spirit of God is moving with mighty power. Many of you are on the verge of a decision for Christ. Don't let the fear of man frighten you out of taking your stand now.

Safety

Whoso putteth his trust in Jehovah shall be safe. He will be safe from all danger of yielding to sin and temptation. If you trust God, temptation has no power. A man cannot yield to

---

4   A streptococcal infection.

temptation without distrusting God. Every act of sin is an act of distrust in God. He that trusts God will do what's right though the heavens fall.

I know a man in business in America. This man was unfortunate in business, lost about everything he had, and sold off everything to pay his honest debts. He kept from failing; he paid all his debts, but it left him practically penniless. Then an opening came for him as fireman on an engine. He came to me and said, "What shall I do? I have wanted to be an engine driver for years. They say they will promote me quickly, but if I take this post on a switch engine, I must work on Sundays. What shall I do?"

I said, "Well, you will have to decide for yourself, but if you can't do it with a clear conscience, you can't afford to do it."

He said, "I can't do it with a clear conscience." He refused the position, though he did not know what he could do to support himself and his wife and family of three or four children. A day or two later he got a position that paid only a dollar a day, only four shillings, which is a very small wage. In a few days, he got a position that paid seventy-five dollars per month, and today he is head bookkeeper of one of the biggest mercantile establishments in the Northwest, with a big salary and constantly getting presents from the firm – all because he trusted God.

When I was home this summer, I found that a young Jewish woman had been converted. She was a very brilliant woman in her work – a very talented woman – but she had to work for her living to support the family. After she was converted, she was full of love for Christ, as Jews generally are when they are converted. As she went out of the place where she worked, a very large establishment – all you businessmen would know the firm by name if I should name it – she spoke of Christ to the other employees. Some of them did not like it, and they went to the head of the firm and said, "Miss So-and-so is constantly talking to us about Christ. We don't like it."

They called her in and said, "We have no objection to Christianity and no objection to your being a Christian. It is a good thing, but you must not talk about it around this establishment."

"Very well," she said. "I won't work where I can't take Christ with me and talk for my Master." She had a family to support, an aged mother and other members of the family, and did not know where she could go, having just converted from Judaism to Christianity.

"Well, then," they said, "you will have to lose your position."

"Very well," she said. "I will give up my position before I will be disloyal to Jesus Christ."

"Very well," they said. "Go back to your work."

She went back to work. At the end of the week, she got a letter from the firm. She said, "Here is my discharge," and she tore it open.

The head of the establishment said in the letter, "We have a position with great responsibility and with a much larger salary than you are getting. We think you are the woman for the position, and we offer it to you." They saw she could be trusted. Businessmen are looking for individuals whom they can trust.

Safe from All Danger

Whoever trusts in the Lord will be safe from danger of every kind. We read in Romans 8:31: *If God is for us, who is against us?* Men will persecute you. Yes, they will ridicule you. They will do all they can to harm you. Jesus says in John 15:20, *If they persecuted me, they will also persecute you.* They will, but it won't do you any harm. Some people are frightened to death at being persecuted, but it is one of the greatest privileges on earth for converts to be persecuted for Jesus Christ.

In Matthew 5:11-12, Jesus says, *Blessed are ye when men shall reproach you, and persecute you, and shall say all manner of evil against you falsely, for my sake. Rejoice* [not cry, not whine], *and be exceeding glad: for great is your reward in heaven.*

When we were in Ballarat, Australia, there was an organized gang that came to disrupt our meeting. I had said some plain things about dancing, and I had been invited to go to a "decent dance." I went, and what I had said interrupted the dance. They were ashamed to dance, and it destroyed the club; they never had but one dance after that. Anyway, they regretted one invitation that they had sent.

> It is one of the greatest privileges on earth for converts to be persecuted for Jesus Christ.

Well, the dancing element was badly obstructed. If we could stop several hundred of you society people from dancing in this city, it would be a high time. I hope we may have just such a high time. Well, this gang that had organized to disrupt the meetings went way off in the far gallery. The very first night when they came, the power of God came down, and the two ringleaders walked right up from that rear gallery the whole length of the hall; they came down to the front, turned around, and said, "We accept Jesus Christ."

The next day some friends of the ringleader of the two met him on the street, knocked him down, and pounded him to make him swear. But God had taken all the swearing out of him, and instead of swearing, he wrote one of the most beautiful letters – not to me but to a friend of his, who sent it to me – one of the most beautiful letters I ever saw about the joy of suffering for Jesus' sake. Men, they may persecute you. They may pound you and hound you, but they can't hurt you if you are right with God.

Once more, the man who trusts in the Lord is eternally safe. Jesus says in John 10:28-29, *I give unto them eternal life; and they shall never perish, and no one shall snatch them out of my hand. My Father, who hath given them unto me, is greater than all; and no one is able to snatch them out of the Father's hand.*

If you trust in the Lord, then God the Father Almighty's hand is under you and around you; Christ the Son's hand is over you and around you. And there you are between the almighty hand of God the Father and God the Son, and all the devils in hell can't get you.

Throw away your fear of man. In place of it, put your trust in the Lord. You compromising Christians, throw away your compromise. Be totally for God – clean, straight Christians for God. Throw away your guilty silence. Go to work now to bring others to Christ, and continue tomorrow, the next day, and the next day. Throw away your guilty silence about unpopular truth and declare the whole counsel of God, even though they say you are old-fashioned because you tell the truth. And you who are rejecting Christ, throw away your fear; fear not what anybody says but stand up and come forward to accept Christ; confess Him before the world now.

In the early days of Mr. Moody's work in Chicago, there was a man in constant attendance at the services. He seemed for a long time to be on the point of decision for Christ. At last Mr. Moody went to him and urged him very strongly to decide at once. He replied that he could not appear as a Christian. He said there was a man with whom he was associated who would ridicule him, and he could not endure his ridicule.

As Mr. Moody kept urging him to decide, the man at last became irritated and quit attending the church. Some months later, when the man had dropped out of sight, Mr. Moody received an urgent call to go and see the man at once. He found him very ill, apparently dying, and in great anxiety about his soul. He was shown the way of life and professed to accept Christ, and his soul seemed at rest.

To everyone's surprise, he took a turn for the better, and a full recovery seemed sure. Mr. Moody called upon him and found him sitting outside in the sunshine. Mr. Moody said, "Now that you have accepted Christ, and God has raised you up, you will certainly come and confess Him as soon as you are able to come back."

To Mr. Moody's astonishment the man replied, "No, not now. I don't dare reveal this in Chicago, but I am intending soon to move to Michigan; as soon as I get there, I will come out publicly and take my stand on the side of Christ."

Mr. Moody told him that Christ could preserve him in Chicago as well as in Michigan, but the man's fear of his friend held him back; he refused to take his stand in Chicago. Mr. Moody left, greatly disappointed. Just one week from that day, the man's wife called upon Mr. Moody and begged him to come at once and see her husband; he had suffered a relapse and was worse than ever. A council of physicians had agreed that there was no possibility of recovery.

"Did he send for me to come?" asked Mr. Moody.

"No. He says that he is lost, and there is no hope for him. He does not wish to see you or speak to you, but I cannot let him die in this way. You must come."

Mr. Moody hurried to the house and found the man in a state of utter despair. To all Mr. Moody's pleas for him to receive Christ then and there, he replied that it was too late, that he was lost, that he had thrown away his day of opportunity, and that he could not be saved now.

Mr. Moody said, "I will pray for you."

"No," said the man, "don't pray for me. It is no use; I am lost. Pray for my wife and children. They need your prayers."

Mr. Moody knelt down by his side and prayed, but the heavens above his head seemed as brass. His own prayers did not seem to go higher than his head. He could not connect with God for this man's salvation. When he arose, the man said, "There, Mr. Moody, I knew that prayer would do no good; I am lost."

With a heavy heart, Mr. Moody left the house. All the afternoon the man kept repeating, *The harvest is past, the summer is ended, and [I am] not saved* (Jeremiah 8:20). All afternoon he kept repeating this text. As the sun was setting behind the western prairies, the man passed away. In his last moments, they heard him whispering, and leaning over to catch his words, they heard him murmuring, *The harvest is past, the summer is ended, and [I am] not saved.* Another soul went out into eternity unprepared, snared into eternal hell by the fear of man. I beg you, throw away your fear of man, and put your trust in the Lord; be saved right now.

Chapter 13

How God Loved the World

For God so loved the world, that he gave his only begotten Son, that whosoever believeth on him should not perish, but have eternal life. (John 3:16)

God has given me that verse of Scripture for my next text, which I suppose has been used for the salvation of more people than any other verse in the Bible. It is John 3:16: *For God so loved the world, that he gave his only begotten Son, that whosoever believeth on him should not perish, but have eternal life.* Thousands of people have been saved by that wonderful verse – tens of thousands, even hundreds of thousands, by simply reading it in the Bible, seeing it painted on a wall, or having it presented to them on a piece of cardboard.

If there were time, I could tell you of a boy who started to read the Bible through and was brought under deep conviction of sin. As he read on and on, he came to the New Testament and to the Gospel of John, to the third chapter and the sixteenth verse, where he read: *For God so loved the world, that he gave his only begotten Son, that whosoever believeth on him should not perish, but have eternal life.* And the moment he saw it, he saw Christ on the cross for his sins, his burden all rolled away, and he found peace. I hope that hundreds will be converted through my text.

This text tells us some important things about the love of God. It tells us that our salvation begins with God's love. We are not saved because we love God; we are saved because God extends His love toward us. Our salvation begins with God's extending His love to us, and it ends with our loving God.

God's Love Is Extended to All

The first thing our text teaches us about the love of God is that the love of God is extended to all. *God so loved the world* – not some part of it, not some elect people, not some select class – but *God so loved the world.* God extends His love to the rich, but God extends His love to the poor just as much as He does to the rich. If one of the wealthiest men or women in this city should come and accept Christ when I give the invitation, many of you would be greatly pleased. So would I, for the rich need to hear the gospel just as much as the poor, and they are not as likely to do so.

God extends His love to the educated, but God extends his love to the uneducated just as much.

But if some poor man should come, some man who doesn't have a penny or a place to sleep tonight, and receive Christ, many of you would not think it amounted to much. But God would be just as pleased to see the poorest man or woman accept Christ, as He would be to see the richest millionaire that you have in this city accept Him.

God extends His love to the educated, but God extends his love to the uneducated just as much. God extends His love to the great scholar, the man of science, the university professor, and the student, but God extends His love to the man who can't read or write just as much as He extends His love to the most brilliant scientist or philosopher on earth. If one of your university professors was to be converted, some of you would be delighted. You would say, "Oh, a wonderful thing happened. One of our learned professors was converted." But if some man or woman who can't even read or write accepts Christ, some of you would not think it meant much, but God would be just as pleased as He would be over the conversion of that university professor. But the most wonderful thing of all is this – God extends His love to the moral, the upright, the virtuous, and the righteous, and God just as truly extends His love to the sinner, the outcast, the abandoned, and the immoral; He extends his love to the bad and the good. *God commendeth his own love toward us, in that, while we were yet sinners, Christ died for us* (Romans 5:8).

I was preaching one night in the city of Minneapolis. It was a hot summer's night, so hot that all the window frames had been taken out at the back to let a little fresh air in; the room was packed. Way down at the back of the room, a man was sitting where the window frame had been taken out, and when I gave the invitation for all who wished to be saved that night and told them to hold up their hands, that man sitting in the window raised his hand. But as soon as I pronounced the benediction, he started for the door. I forgot all about my discussion after the meeting. I don't know to this day what became of that discussion. All I saw was that man starting for the door, and I hurried after him. I caught him just as he turned to descend the stairway. I laid my hand on his shoulder as he turned the corner. I said to him, "My friend, you held up your hand to say you wanted to be saved."

"Yes, I did."

"Why didn't you stay, then, for the second meeting?"

He said, "It is no use."

"Why?" I said. "God loves you."

He said, "You don't know who you are talking to."

I said, "I don't care who I am talking to. I know God loves you."

He said, "I am the meanest thief in Minneapolis."

"Well," I said, "if you are the meanest thief in Minneapolis, I can prove to you from the Bible that God loves you." I opened my Bible to Romans 5:8 and read: "*God commendeth his own love toward us, in that, while we were yet sinners, Christ died for us.* Now," I said, "if you are the meanest thief in Minneapolis, you are certainly a sinner, and that verse says that God loves sinners."

It broke the man's heart, and he commenced to weep. I took him to my office, and we sat down, and he told me his story. He said, "I am just out of confinement. I was released from prison this morning. I had started out this evening with some companions that I knew had committed one of the most daring burglaries that was ever committed in this city, and by tomorrow morning, I would either have had a big stake of money or a bullet in my body. But as we were going down the street, we passed the corner where you were holding that open-air meeting. You had a Scotsman speaking. My mother was Scottish, and when I heard that Scottish tongue, it reminded me of my mother. The other night in prison I had a dream about my mother. I dreamed that my mother came to me and begged me to give up my wicked life, and when I heard that Scotsman talk, I stepped up to listen. My two pals said, 'Come along,' and cursed me. I said, 'I am going to listen to what this man says.' Then they tried to drag me across the street, but I would not go. What that man said touched my heart, and when you gave the invitation to the meeting, I came, and that is why I am here."

I opened my Bible, and I showed that man from the Bible that God extends His love towards sinners; I showed him how

Christ had died for sinners and how he could be saved by simply accepting Christ. And then and there, he did accept Christ. We knelt down side by side, and that man offered the one of the most wonderful prayers I ever heard in all my life.

Is there a thief here? God extends His love to you. Is there a pickpocket here? God extends His love to you. Is there a lost woman here? God extends His love to you. Is there an infidel here? God extends His love to you. Is there a blasphemer here? God extends His love to you. I will tell you something you can't find in all the city. You can't find a man or woman that God doesn't offer His love to.

God's Love Is Holy

The second thing our text teaches us about the love of God is that it is a holy love. *God so loved the world, that he gave his only begotten Son.* Many people cannot understand that. They say, "I cannot see why it is that if God loves me, He doesn't forgive my sins outright without His Son dying in my place. I cannot see the necessity of Christ's death. If God is love, and if God loves me and loves everybody, why doesn't He take us to heaven right away without Christ dying for us?"

You can't find a man or woman that God doesn't offer His love to.

The text answers the question: *God so loved – so* loved. That *so* brings out in what way that God loved the world. It was of such a character that God could not and would not pardon sin without an atonement. God is a holy God. God's love is a holy love. God's holiness, like everything in God, is real. There is no sham in God. It is real love, real righteousness, and real holiness, and God's holiness, since it is real, must manifest itself in some way. Either it must manifest itself in the punishment of the sinner – in our eternal banishment from Him, in your ruin and in mine – or it must manifest itself in some other way. The atoning death of Jesus Christ on the cross of Calvary was God substituting His atoning action – whereby He expressed His hatred of sin – for the punishment whereby He would have expressed the same thing.

But some man says, "That is not just. The doctrine you teach is that God took the sin of man and laid it upon Jesus Christ, who was innocent, and that is not just."

Well, that might not seem just, but that is what the Bible teaches, and that is what I teach. No ordinary man could have died for you and me. It would have been of no value. But Jesus Christ was the second Adam, the second head of the race, the second person, your representative and mine. When Christ died on the cross of Calvary, I died in Him through my faith in Him, and the penalty of my sin was paid.

The philosophy of the atonement as laid down in the Bible is the most profound and wonderful philosophy the world has ever seen or heard. The Christian doctrine is a perfect whole. If you take out one doctrine, the others are irrational; but if you put them all together, they are a perfect system. For example, if you become a Unitarian and remove the deity of Christ, the atonement becomes irrational. If you remove the humanity of Christ and have Jesus Christ as merely divine, the atonement becomes irrational. But if you take all that the Bible says, that God was in Christ, and that in Christ the Word became flesh, real man, God manifest in the flesh, then the atonement of Christ is the most profoundly and wonderfully philosophical truth the world has ever seen.

God's love was a holy love. I thank God that it was. I thank God that His method was such that in perfect righteousness, perfect justice, perfect holiness, as well as perfect love, He could pardon and save the vilest of sinners on the ground of Christ's atoning death. And when you gain a proper sense of your sinfulness and see God as He really is, nothing will satisfy your conscience. Nothing can do that except the doctrine that God, the Holy One, substituted His atoning action whereby He expressed His hatred of sin, for His punitive action whereby He would have expressed the same hatred of sin, and in the death of Jesus Christ on the cross of Calvary, your sin and mine was perfectly settled forever.

Thank God, the broken law of God has no claim on me. I broke it, I admit it; but Jesus Christ kept it, and having kept it, He satisfied its punitive claim by dying for those who had not kept it. On the ground of that atoning death, there is pardon for the vilest sinner.

A man sits here and says, "There is no forgiveness for me." Why not? "Because I have descended deep into sin."

Listen, men. You have descended deep into sin; you have gone deeper into sin than you realize yourself, but while your sins are as high as the mountains, the atonement that covers them is as high as heaven. While your sins are as deep as the ocean, the atonement that swallows them is as deep as eternity. On the ground of Christ's atoning death, there is pardon for the vilest sinner on the face of this earth.

The Greatness of God's Love

The third thing our text teaches us about the love of God is the greatness of that love. *God so loved the world, that he gave his only begotten Son, that whosoever believeth on him should not perish, but have eternal life.* The greatness of God's love appears in two ways in the text: first, in the greatness of the gift He offers us – eternal life. It does not mean merely a life that is endless in its duration. Thank God, it means that, but it means more; it means a life that is perfect and divine in its quality as well as endless in its duration is what is offered to you now. *God so loved the world, that he gave his only begotten Son, that who-soever believeth on him should not perish, but have eternal life.*

I do thank God for a life that is perfect in quality and that will never end. Most of us will die before long, as far as our physical life is concerned. A large number of the eight or nine thousand people who are listening to my voice will be in their graves in a few months – more of us in a year, more in five, still more in ten, almost all of us in forty. Eighty years from today, there probably won't be a person on this earth who is here now, unless the Lord has returned. Well, you say, eighty years is a long time for you young people. No, it is not. It looks long to look forward to, but when you get to be forty-eight, as I am, and there are only thirty-two years of it left, it does not look very long. It looks very short. Eighty years doesn't look very long, and when the eighty years are up, what then?

Suppose I had a guarantee today that I was going to live two hundred years in perfect health, strength, and prosperity. Would that satisfy me? No, it would not, for what happens when the two hundred years are up? Suppose I had a guarantee today that I was to live a thousand years in perfect health and strength and prosperity. Would that satisfy me? No, it would not, for what happens when the thousand years are up? Suppose I had a guarantee today that I would live on this earth for ten thousand years in perfect health and strength and prosperity. Would that satisfy me? No, it would not, for what happens when the ten thousand years are up?

> I want something that never ends, and, thank God, in Christ I have something that never ends.

I want something that never ends, and, thank God, in Christ I have something that never ends. Thousands of years will pass into tens of thousands; tens of thousands will pass into millions; millions will pass into hundreds of millions; hundreds of millions will pass into billions; and the billions will pass into trillions. And I will be living on and on in ever-growing joy and glory. Eternal life! Who can have it? Anybody. *Whosoever believeth on him.*

What does *whosoever* mean? Somebody asked a little boy once, "What does *whosoever* mean?"

The little fellow answered, "It means you and me and everybody else."

Thank God, it does. It means you and me and everybody else. Somebody (I think it was John Bradford) once said that he was glad that John 3:16 did not read that "God so loved the world, that He gave His only begotten Son that John Bradford might have everlasting life. Because," he said, "if it read that way, I would be afraid it meant some other John Bradford. But when I read that *God so loved the world, that he gave his only begotten Son, that whosoever believeth on him,* I know that means me." Thank God, it did, and it means everybody else too.

I came here with a pocket quite well filled with shillings, half-crowns, half-sovereigns, sovereigns, and checks that have come to me through the mail today. They are all gone. I handed them all over to the treasurer. But now while I go out with an empty pocket, I will go out with a full heart – a heart that is full of everlasting life – and that is worth millions of sovereigns. Every other man and woman can go out the same way.

But the text tells us another more wonderful way in which the greatness of the love of God shows itself, and that is in the sacrifice that God made for us. *God so loved the world, that he gave his only begotten Son.* Now, as I said before, the measure of love is sacrifice. You can tell just how much anybody loves you by the sacrifice that he is willing to make for you. God has shown the measure of His love by the sacrifice He made. What was it? His very best. He *so loved the world, that he gave his only begotten Son,* the dearest thing that He had. No earthly father ever loved his son as God loved Jesus Christ. I have an only son; how I love him. My wife and I have often wished that God in His kindness had given us three or four sons, provided they were all like the one He gave us, just as He has given us four daughters. But this thought occurred to me this afternoon – that perhaps the reason God only gave us one son was that I might have a little deeper realization of how much God loved Jesus Christ.

Suppose someday I should see that boy of mine arrested; suppose we went as a missionaries to China, and I saw him arrested by the enemies of Christ. Suppose they blindfolded him, spit in his face, punched him in the face, braided a crown of big cruel thorns and put it on his brow, and then some Chinese man came along and knocked that crown down on his brow until the blood poured down his face on either side. How do you suppose I would feel?

Then suppose they took him, stripped his garments from him, took him to a post, made him lean over until the skin of his back was all drawn tight. Suppose they bound him to the post, and a soldier came along and lashed the boy's back thirty-nine times with a long stick that had long lashes of leather attached to it in which were twisted bits of brass and lead. Suppose he lashed him until he was all torn and bleeding, and his back was one mass of bloody wounds. How do you think I would feel?

Then suppose they laid a cross down upon the ground and stretched his right hand out on the arm of the cross, put a nail in the hand, lifted the heavy hammer, and drove the nail through the hand. Then they stretched his left arm on the other arm of the cross, put a nail in the palm of that hand, lifted the heavy hammer, and drove the nail through that hand. Then they put a nail on his feet, lifted the heavy hammer, and drove the nail through his feet. They took that cross to which he was nailed and plunged it into a hole on a rock and left him hanging there, the agony getting worse and worse every minute.

I see him hanging there beneath the burning sun from nine o'clock in the morning until three o'clock in the afternoon and watch as my only boy dies in awful agony on a cross. How do you suppose I would feel?

But that is just what God saw. He loved His only begotten Son, as you and I never dreamed of loving our sons. He saw them spit in His face; He saw them blindfold Him; He saw them strike Him with their fists. He saw them beat Him with rods; He saw them take the crown of awful thorns, press it on His brow, and then smack it down with a heavy rod. He saw them strip the garments from His back, tie Him to a post, make Him lean over until the skin upon His back was drawn tight, and allow a brawny Roman soldier to scourge him thirty-nine times until His back was one mass of aching wounds. He saw them take Him and stretch Him on a cross, drive a nail into His hands, drive a nail into His feet, and take that cross and plunge it into a hole on that rock. He saw them leave Him hanging there, aching, all His bones out of joint, tortured in every member of His body! God looked on. Why did He suffer this? Because He loved you and me, and it was the only way that you and I could be saved. *God so loved the world, that he gave his only begotten Son, that whosoever believeth on him should not perish, but have eternal life.*

How are you going to repay that love? I know how some of you are going to repay it. You are going to repay it with hatred. You hate God. You never said it, but it is true.

A friend of mine was preaching one time in Connecticut. He stopped by a physician who had a beautiful, amiable daughter. She had never made a profession of religion, but she was such a beautiful character that people thought she was a Christian. One night, after the meetings had been going on for some time, my friend said to this young lady, "Aren't you going to the meeting tonight?"

She said, "No, Mr. Hammond, I am not."

"Oh," he said, "I think you had better go."

She said, "I will not go."

"Why," he said, "don't you love God?"

She said, "I hate God." She had never realized it before. I think she would have said she loved God up to that time, but when the demands of God were pressed home by the Holy Spirit, she was not willing to obey. She realized that she hated God.

Some of you have never discovered that you hate God, but it is true. How some of you used the name of God today! You have used it many times. In prayer? No, in profanity. Why? Because you hate God. Some of you men, if your wives should receive Christ, you would make life unendurable. Why? Because you hate God, and you are going to make your wife miserable for accepting His Son. Some of you young people, if some other young person in your shop, factory, or mill should accept Christ, you would laugh at them. Why? Because you hate God. Some of you people will read every secular book you can get or go to every secular lecture. You are trying to convince yourself that the Bible is not God's Word, and if anybody would come along and mention some smart objection to the Bible, you would laugh at it and rejoice in it. Why? Because you hate God, and you want to get rid of God's Book. Some of you love to hold up your heads and toss them and say, "I don't believe in the divinity of Christ; I don't believe He is the Son of God." Why? Because you hate God, and if you can rob His divine Son of the honor that belongs to Him, you will do it. You are repaying the wondrous love of God with hate.

Some of you are refusing to accept Christ. You attend a mission service night after night, but when people speak to you, you get angry. You say, "I wish you wouldn't talk to me. Go about

> Some of you have never discovered that you hate God, but it is true.

your own business. It is none of your business whether I am a Christian or not." You get angry every time anybody speaks to you. Why? Because you hate God.

Some of you so bitterly hate God that you are trying to find fault with the doctrine of the atonement. You are trying to make yourself believe that Christ did not die on the cross for you. You say, "I cannot understand the philosophy of it." If you loved God, you would not stop to ask about the philosophy of it. You would simply lift your heart in simple gratitude and praise to God that He so loved you that He gave His Son to die for you.

Conquering Power of God's Love

There is one other thing that our text teaches us about the love of God, and that is the conquering power of His love. *God so loved the world, that he gave his only begotten Son, that who-soever believeth on him should not perish, but have eternal life.* The love of God conquers sin; the love of God conquers death; the love of God conquers wrong and saves a man from perishing unto everlasting life. And the love of God conquers where everything else fails.

The first time I ever preached in Chicago was several years before I went there to live. I was there at a convention after the sermon among the people who stood up that night to say they wanted to be prayed for. I noticed a young woman who did not come forward when the rest came. I went down to where she was standing and urged her to come forward. She laughed and said, "No, I am not going forward," and sat down again.

The next night was not an evangelistic service but a meeting of the convention. I was president of the convention. As I looked over the audience toward the back, I saw that young woman, elegantly dressed – likely the most finely dressed woman in the audience. I called somebody else to the chair and slipped around to the back part of the building. When the meeting was dismissed, I made my way to where that young lady was sitting. I sat down beside her. I said, "Won't you receive Christ tonight?"

"No," she said. "Would you like to know the kind of life I am living?"

It was not known that she was living that kind of life. She was living it in the best society, honored and respected. Then she commenced to unfold to me one of the saddest stories of dishonor without blushing, laughing as if it were a good joke. Finally she said, "Let me tell you how I spent last Easter."

I cannot tell you how it was, how any woman with any sense could have told it to any man I cannot imagine. When she had told the story, she burst out into a laugh and said, "That was a funny way to spend Easter, wasn't it?"

I was dumbfounded. I simply took my Bible, opened it to John 3:16, passed it to her, and said, "Won't you please read that?"

She had to hold it very near her eyes to see the print, and she began in a laughing way. "*God so loved.*" She was laughing no more. "*The world.*" There was nothing like a laugh now. "*That he gave his only begotten Son.*" And she burst into tears, and the tears literally dripped onto the elegant silk robe that she was wearing. Hardened as she was, brazen as she was, shameless as she was, trifling as she was, one glimpse of Jesus on the cross of Calvary for her had broken her heart. God grant that it may break your hearts.

I want to tell you of one more incident. One night I was preaching, and we had a discussion after the meeting. The leading soprano in my choir was not a Christian. I don't believe in having an unconverted choir member; we don't allow anybody in our choir in Chicago who is not a converted person to the best of our knowledge. You say, "You must have a pretty small choir." We have two hundred, and every one of them, as far as we know, is converted. But in the church where I was preaching that night, it was not so, and my leading soprano was not a Christian. She was a happy, worldly girl but not really immoral. She was a generally respectable girl yet very worldly, and yet mostly cheerful. She stayed for the discussion after the meeting. Her mother stood in the middle of the house and said, "I wish you would all pray for the conversion of my daughter."

I did not look around at the choir, but I knew perfectly well how that young woman looked without seeing her. I knew her cheeks were burning; I knew her eyes were flashing; and I knew that she was angry from the crown of her head to the soles of her feet. As soon as the meeting was over, I hurried to the particular door that I knew she would have to pass by. As she came along, I stepped toward her, held out my hand, and said, "Good evening, Cora."

Her eyes flashed, and her cheeks burned. She did not take my hand. She stomped her foot and said, "Mr. Torrey, my mother knows better than to do what she has done tonight. She knows it will only make me worse."

I said, "Cora, sit down."

The angry girl sat down. I opened my Bible to Isaiah 53:5 and handed it to her. I said, "Won't you please read it?"

And she read: *"He was wounded for our transgressions, he was bruised for our iniquities; the chastisement of our peace was upon him."* She did not get any further; she burst into tears, for the love of God revealed in the cross of Christ had broken her heart.

I left the city the next day. While I was away, I got a letter saying that this young lady was happily converted but very ill. I returned to Minneapolis, called at the house, and found her rejoicing in Christ but so ill that the physician held out no hope of her recovery.

A few days later, her brother came running up to my house in the morning about ten o'clock. He said, "Mr. Torrey, come to the house as quickly as you can. Cora has been unconscious all the morning. She has not spoken a word. She hardly seems to be breathing. She is as white as marble, and we think she is dying. She seems to be utterly unconscious."

I hurried back to her home. And there lay the whitest living person I had ever seen, bleeding to death through her gums and nose. She was unconscious apparently, and had not said a word all morning. Her mother stood at the foot of the bed with a breaking heart. "Oh," she said, "Mr. Torrey, pray, pray, please pray!"

I knelt down by the bedside and prayed. I didn't imagine the girl could hear a word I said. I was praying to comfort her mother. And just as soon as I had finished my prayer, the most wonderful prayer I have ever heard in my life came from those white lips in a clear, strong, beautiful voice. The dying girl said, "O, heavenly Father, I want to live if it is Your will, so that as I have sung in the past for my own glory, I can sing for the glory of Jesus, who loved me and gave Himself for me. Father, I want to live, but if You do not see fit to raise me up from this bed, I shall be glad to depart and be with Christ." And she departed to be with Christ. The love of God had conquered.

Let the love of God conquer your stubborn, wicked, foolish, sinful, worldly, careless hearts. *God so loved the world, that he gave his only begotten Son, that whosoever believeth on him should not perish, but have eternal life.* Yield to that love now. Amen.

Chapter 14

Today – Tomorrow

The Holy Spirit saith, To-day. (Hebrews 3:7)
Boast not thyself of tomorrow. (Proverbs 27:1)

Today is the wise man's day; tomorrow is the fool's day. The wise man is the man who, when he sees what ought to be done, does it today. The foolish man is the man who, when he sees what ought to be done, says, "I will do it tomorrow." The men who always do today the thing they see ought to be done today are the men who make a success for time and for eternity. The people who put off until tomorrow what ought to be done today are those who make a shipwreck of time and of eternity. *The Holy Spirit saith, To-day.* In the folly of his heart, man says, "Tomorrow."

I will give you five reasons why every truly wise man who has not already accepted Christ as his Savior, surrendered to Him as his Lord and Master, and openly confessed Him as such before the world will do it now. I have no doubt that there are literally hundreds, if not thousands, who intend to be Christians sometime, but who keep saying, "Not yet," "Not today." I will tell you not merely why you ought to become Christians but also why you ought to become Christians now.

Find Joy Sooner

First: The sooner you come to Christ the sooner you will find the wonderful joy which is to be found in Him. Without question, in Jesus Christ is an immeasurably better joy than there is in the world – a purer joy, a higher joy, a holier joy, a more satisfying joy, a more abiding joy, a more wonderful joy in every way. This fact is indisputable. Everyone who keeps his eyes open knows that it is true. Go to any person who has ever tried the world and tried Christ, and ask him which joy is better – the joy he found in the world or the joy he has found in Christ. You will get the same answer every time.

Jesus Christ is an immeasurably better joy than there is in the world.

The joy found in the world is not for a moment to be compared with the joy that is found in Christ. I have tried both. I have had abundant opportunity to try both. If ever a person had an opportunity to try what this world can give, I had it, and I tried it. I tried all that could be found in the world; then I turned to Christ and tried Him, and my testimony is like the testimony of millions of others who have found that the joy of the world is nothing and the joy in Christ is everything. I don't care how fully a person may have gone into the joys of this world, or how great his opportunity may have been to test them. Go to anybody who has tried both, and you cannot find in all the world a man who has found Christ and not tell you there is a joy in Christ higher, deeper, broader, wider, longer, more wonderful in every way than the joy that the world gives. Well, the sooner you come to Christ, the sooner you will have that joy.

Escape Misery Sooner

Second: The sooner you come to Christ, the sooner you will escape the wretchedness and misery that there is away from Christ. There is misery in an accusing conscience. No one who is without Christ has peace of conscience. One night I was preaching to an audience of men and women to whom a twenty-dollar gold piece would have been a great help. I put my hand in my pocket as I was preaching, and I felt the twenty-dollar gold piece. I took it out and held it up and said, "Now, if there is a man in this audience who is without Christ and has peace in his heart, deep, abiding satisfaction and rest, who will come up here and say so, I will give him this twenty-dollar gold piece." Nobody came up.

When the meeting was over, I stood at the door with the twenty-dollar gold piece, for I thought they might be timid about coming forward for it. I said, "If anybody can claim this twenty dollars on the conditions I have named, who can say, 'I have peace of conscience and heart. My heart is satisfied without Christ,' he can have this twenty-dollar gold piece."

They filed out, and nobody claimed the gold piece. Finally, a man came along, and I said, "Don't you want this twenty dollars?"

"But," he said, "I cannot claim it on those conditions." Neither can you.

Another night I was preaching in Chicago, and I asked everybody in the building who had found rest and perfect satisfaction through the acceptance of Christ to stand up. Hundreds of men and women, more than a thousand, rose to their feet. Then I asked them to sit down, and I said, "If there is an unbeliever in this house who can say he has found rest, peace, and perfect satisfaction in his unbelief, will he please stand?"

There were many unbelievers present. One man got up in the gallery, and I said, "I see a gentleman up there. I am glad he has the courage of his convictions. I would like to speak with him in the discussion time after the meeting."

He came to the discussion. I said, "Mr. S., you stood up in the meeting tonight to say that you had perfect rest and peace without Christ and that your soul was satisfied with unbelief. Was that true?"

"Oh," he said, "Mr. Torrey, that will have to be qualified." I guess it will. *There is no peace, saith Jehovah, to the wicked* (Isaiah 48:22).

Then there is the slavery of sin away from Christ. *Every one that committeth sin is the bondservant of sin* (John 8:34). Without Christ there is dread of what may happen, dread of disaster, dread of what man may do, and dread of what may be beyond the grave. When you come to Christ, you get rid of fear of man. You have no fear of misfortune, for you are able to say, *To them that love God all things work together for good* (Romans 8:28). You have no fear of death, for what men call death is simply to depart and be with Christ.

By coming to Christ, you get rid of all this wretchedness; you get rid of the accusations of conscience; you get rid of the slavery of sin; you get rid of all dread of disaster; and you get rid of the dread of death the moment you accept Christ. Why not get rid of it all?

Suppose you were on the shore and saw a shipwreck in the distance with a man clinging to it, and cold waters sweeping over him every little while. It was a cold wintry night, and you and others go out in a lifeboat and say to him, "We have come to rescue you. Drop into the lifeboat."

Suppose the man would say, "No, I think I can hold on until morning; come out again in the morning, and I will get into the boat and come ashore."

You would say, "Man, are you mad? Why stay out here tonight when you can come ashore now?"

Out on the shipwreck, every little while the cold waves break over you. All the wretchedness of an accusing conscience, the bondage of sin, the fear of possible death, and the soul away from God beats upon you. Why cling to the wreck another night, when you can come ashore to safety and joy now, if you will drop right into the lifeboat?

Accomplish More for Christ

Third: The sooner you come to Christ, the more you can do for Christ. The moment a person is saved, he wants to do something for the Master. If you are saved a year from today, you will go to work for Christ, but there will be one year gone that will never come back – the year between now and a year from now (if you come in a year from now). You can never go back over this year. You are associated with friends that you can lead to Christ between now and a year from now who may be beyond your reach then. Before I was converted, I had a friend, and we were often together. We lived in the same building. We went pleasuring together. If I had been a Christian, I could have led him to Christ.

Three years later, after I had accepted Christ, that young man passed beyond my reach. The day I went back to the university to study for my second degree, my father picked up *The New York Herald* and read about a young man who was out playing ball. The man out in center field threw the ball. This young man's back was toward the center field, and he was struck at the base of the brain; he never regained consciousness. As my father read this and came to the name, he said, "Archie, isn't that your old friend?"

I took the paper and read it. I said, "Yes, it is my old friend." Called into eternity without a moment's warning, and my opportunity of bringing him to Christ was gone forever. How often in the years that have come since, and God has used me to lead others to Christ, I have thought back to Frank. In spite of all those who are now coming to Christ, Frank is gone, and my opportunity of saving him lost forever.

If you postpone receiving Christ for thirty days, people that you might have reached during those thirty days will have passed beyond your reach forever.

In my first pastorate, a woman who was a little over fifty and had been a backslider was saved. She became the best worker in all the community, but her own two sons had grown up during the years when she was far from God. They had both married and passed beyond her reach. Though she has been used to bring many to Christ, she has never been able to bring these two sons to Christ. Her day of opportunity for them was while she was living in the world. Fathers and mothers, if you are far from God and not saved, you may be saved some other day, but these sons and daughters that you might bring with you, if you come now, will likely have passed beyond your reach forever. The sooner you come to Christ, the more you can bring with you, so come today.

> The sooner you come to Christ, the more you can bring with you, so come today.

Attain a Richer Eternity

Fourth: The sooner you come to Christ, the richer will be your eternity. We are saved by grace; we are rewarded according to our works. Every day of a man's life after he is saved, he is laying up treasures in heaven, and every day you live for Christ, you will be that much richer for all eternity. Some people have the idea that a man can be saved on his deathbed and have as abundant an entrance into the kingdom of God as he could have if he had been saved for forty years. What nonsense! You have neither common sense nor biblical support for it.

A man may be saved on his deathbed. I won't say that no man ever is; I believe some are, though not very many. A man may be saved on his deathbed, but he is saved *so as through fire* (1 Corinthians 3:15). His works are all burned up, and he enters heaven penniless. The man that is saved forty years before he dies and serves Christ for forty years, every day of those forty years he is making deposits in eternity, for which he will be richer throughout all eternity. *Lay up for yourselves treasures in heaven* (Matthew 6:20).

The sooner you come to Christ, how much fuller your hands will be when you enter the kingdom of God. I thank God I was converted when I was, but what would I give for those six wasted years through which I deliberately resisted the Spirit of God! But I can't call them back.

Avoid Losing the Opportunity

Fifth: The sooner you come to Christ, the surer you are to come to Christ. If you are not saved now, you may be tomorrow, but then again, you may not be. I believe there are scores of people who will be saved now or never. When a person stands on a platform, looks over a vast audience, and feels in his very soul that the eternal salvation of hundreds of souls is trembling in the balances as the result of his sermon, he experiences an awful feeling. That is the feeling I have when I preach. I believe there are hundreds of people that hear every word I am saying who will be saved now or never.

The Spirit of God may leave you. People think they can turn to Christ when they choose, but when the Spirit of God is in the room, passing from seat to seat and heart to heart, it is an awful moment. To say yes means life; to say no means death.

To say yes means heaven; to say no means hell. Often a man will be so near the kingdom, and he will say, "I am so interested I will certainly be just as much interested tomorrow," but the critical hour has come, and if you do not yield now, you may have no interest tomorrow.

I once received a message from a wealthy young fellow in New Haven, Connecticut, saying that he wished to see me that night at Mr. Moody's meeting. I went and met him at the close of the meeting. He was on the verge of a decision. As we stood talking in Chapel Street Church, the college bell rang out at a late hour. I thought he was so near a decision that I could leave him safely until morning. So I said, "Good-night, Will. I'll be around to your room tomorrow morning at ten."

That was one of the most fatal mistakes I ever made. I was there at ten, and he was there, but his convictions had vanished. He was as hard as flint. His opportunity had come and gone. You may be very near a decision, but if you say no now, tomorrow may be forever too late.

Who of us can tell who will be called out of the world into eternity in a moment? At our first men's meeting in the Empire Theatre in Edinburgh, a Roman Catholic young man accepted Christ. Little did he or we realize that it was his last chance. The next day he was hurried to the infirmary for an operation, and the operation proved fatal. By accepting Christ at that meeting, he was just in time. If he had waited a day, he would have been lost forever.

> The sooner you come to Christ, the richer you will be throughout all eternity.

You have a chance today. Don't throw it away. The sooner you take Christ, the surer you will be to take Him. Receive Him now. You can have the joy of salvation now; why wait a week? You can be saved from a life of wretchedness away from Christ. Why endure it another week? The sooner you come to Christ, the more you can do for Christ. Why not come to Him today? The sooner you come to Christ, the richer you will be throughout all eternity. Why not come to Him now and begin to lay up treasures in the bank of heaven? The sooner you come to Christ, the surer it is that you will come. Come now. *The Holy Spirit saith, To-day* (Hebrews 3:7). *Boast not thyself of tomorrow; for thou knowest not what a day may bring forth* (Proverbs 27:1).

Chapter 15

He That Winneth Souls Is Wise

He that is wise winneth souls. (Proverbs 11:30)

If I should go up and down the streets of this city and ask men and women, "Whom do you regard as the wise man?" I would get a great variety of answers. I might go into some banks and ask the manager, "Whom do you regard as the wise man?" He would likely say, "I regard the man who succeeds in getting the most money as the wise man. I would regard the man who by virtue of rare business intelligence and unusual industry amasses a fortune of first a thousand pounds, then ten thousand pounds, then a hundred thousand pounds, then a million pounds, and then two, three, four, five, or ten million pounds."

If I should go into a political office, I would get a different answer. Very likely the man would reply, "I regard the man who studies the economic and political problems of the day until he has mastered them and succeeds in discovering what is best for his country's financial welfare as a wise man. He wins the confidence of his fellow citizens who elect him to parliament;

he may then be made a cabinet minister and later become prime minister. I regard him as the wise man."

If I should go to military men, I would get a different answer. Very likely the reply would be like this: "I regard the man who masters the art of war, who studies the science of tactics and maneuvers until he knows how to maneuver great forces on the field of battle and lead them to victory. He would first become a captain, then a major, a lieutenant colonel, a colonel, a brigadier general, a major general, a lieutenant general, and finally a field marshal. I regard him as the wise man."

If I should go to young people, I would get another answer. They would likely say, "I regard the man or woman who gets the most pleasure out of life and finds the most fun by day and the most amusement by night as the wise man."

But when I turn away from men with all these conflicting answers and look to God and say, "Heavenly Father, whom do You regard as the wise man?" there comes thundering down from yonder throne of eternal light this answer: *He that is wise winneth souls.* Not he that wins money, not he that wins political distinctions and honor and position, not he that wins fame in the field of battle, and not he that wins the most sport and amusement in life, but he that wins the most men and women to a saving knowledge of Jesus Christ – he is the wise man.

In the eyes of God the wise man is the man who makes soul winning the business of his life, and my main proposition today is that every follower of Jesus Christ should make the winning of others to Christ the business of his life. I know that some of you say, "I don't believe that; I believe that statement is altogether too strong." I am going to give you six unanswerable reasons

> In the eyes of God the wise man is the man who makes soul winning the business of his life.

why soul winning should be the business of life on the part of every follower of Jesus Christ.

Jesus Commanded It

First, soul winning should be the business of every Christian because Jesus Christ has commanded us to do it. When the Lord Jesus Christ left this earth, He left His marching orders with the church. Matthew 28:19 says, *Go ye therefore, and make disciples of all the nations.* That commandment was not merely for the first twelve disciples; it was also for every follower of Jesus Christ in every age of the church's history. If you consider the book of Acts, you will see that in the early church every Christian considered that the Great Commission to make disciples, to win souls, was for himself. For example, if you turn to Acts 8:4, you will read these words: *They therefore that were scattered abroad went about preaching the word.* These that were scattered abroad were not the apostles but the rank and file, the ordinary everyday members of the church.

Some years ago, when I was speaking in the city of Minneapolis, I noticed a young lawyer in the audience. When the meeting was over, I made my way to him and said, "Are you a Christian?"

"Well, sir," he said, "I consider myself a Christian."

I said, "Are you bringing other men to Christ?"

He said, "No, I am not; that is not my business; that's your business; I am not called to do that. I am called to practice law; you are called to preach the gospel."

I said, "If you are called to be a Christian, you are called to bring other men to Christ."

He said, "I don't believe that."

I said, "Look here." Then I opened my Bible to Acts 8:4 and asked him to read.

He read: "*They therefore that were scattered abroad went*

about preaching the word. Oh yes," he said, "but these were the apostles."

I said, "Will you be kind enough to read the first verse of the chapter?"

He read: *"They were all scattered abroad throughout the regions of Judaea and Samaria, except the apostles,"* and *"they therefore that were scattered abroad went about preaching the word."* He had nothing more to say. What could he say?

Every man and every woman who believes they are Christians but is not winning others to Christ is disobedient to Jesus Christ. It is serious business in war to be disobedient to your commanding officer, and it is serious business for a Christian to be disobedient to Jesus Christ. Jesus says, *Ye are my friends, if ye do the things which I command you* (John 15:14). One evening I was told that a minister's son was to be present in my congregation and that though he professed to be a Christian, he did not work much at it. I watched for him and selected the right man from the audience. At the close of the service, I hurried to the door by which he would leave and shook hands with many as they passed outside. When he came to the door, I took his hand and said, "Good evening, I am glad to see you; are you a friend of Jesus?"

"Yes," he replied heartily, "I consider myself a friend of Jesus."

"Jesus says," I replied, *"Ye are my friends, if ye do the things which I command you."*

His eyes fell. "If those are the conditions, I guess I am not."

I put the same question to you: Are you a friend of Jesus? Are you doing whatever He commands you? Are you winning souls as He commands? If I should ask every friend of Jesus to arise, could you conscientiously get up?

Soul Winning Was the Business of Jesus

In the second place, soul winning should be the business of every Christian because it was the business of Jesus Christ Himself. What is it to be a Christian? To be a Christian is to be a follower of Christ. What is it to be a follower of Christ? To be a follower of Christ is to have the same purpose in life that Jesus Christ had. What was Christ's purpose in life? He Himself defines it in Luke 19:10. He says, *The Son of man came to seek and to save that which was lost.* The Lord Jesus Christ had just one purpose in coming down to this earth.

> To be a follower of Christ is to have the same purpose in life that Jesus Christ had.

He had just one purpose in leaving the glory of heaven for the shame of earth. There was just one thing He lived for, one thing He suffered for, one thing He died for – that was to save the lost.

Is that your purpose? Is that what you live for? Is that the one great ambition of your life? Is that the all-absorbing passion of your life? If it is not, what right do you have to call yourself a Christian? If Christ had one purpose in life and you have an entirely different purpose in life, what right do you have to call yourself a follower of Jesus Christ? Jesus Christ says in Matthew 4:19, *Follow me, and I will make you fishers of men.* Are you following Christ? Are you fishing for men? Suppose I had asked at the beginning of this service every follower of Christ to stand up. I think that almost every man and woman in this audience would have stood to their feet. But suppose I now ask every follower of Christ to rise; how many of you could stand up?

Personal Fellowship with Jesus

Third, soul winning should be the business of every Christian because that is where we enjoy the unspeakable privilege of personal fellowship with Jesus Christ. There is a wonderful promise in this Book, one of the most precious promises that it contains, a promise that people constantly quote. I do not wonder that they often quote the promise; what I do wonder is that they quote the promise without reference to the context and the condition. The promise is Matthew 28:20: *Lo, I am with you always, even unto the end of the world.* Is there a more precious promise than that between the covers of this Book? Ah, but notice the condition. You will find it in the preceding verse (v. 19). Jesus said, *Go ye therefore, and make disciples of all the nations, . . . and lo, I am with you always, even unto the end of the world.*

In other words, Jesus says, "You go my way, and I will go yours. You go out with me in fellowship and in work, and I will go out with you in personal fellowship."

I want to ask you a question: Have you any right to this promise? You have often quoted it; you have often built upon it; but have you any right to it? Are you going out as far as your influence extends, making disciples and winning souls? Your influence may not extend very far, but as far as your influence extends, are you going out to bring other men or women to Christ? If you are, you have a right to that promise. If you are not, you have no right to that promise.

To Enjoy the Fullness of the Holy Spirit

Fourth, soul winning should be the business of every one of us, because in that work we enjoy the fullness of the Holy Spirit's presence and power. There is no greater blessing than to receive the Holy Spirit, to be filled with the Holy Spirit, and to be baptized with the Holy Spirit. Oh, the joy of personally receiving and being filled with and baptized with the Holy Spirit! It is heaven come down to earth. But that blessing is given for a specific purpose and can only be acquired for that purpose. That purpose is revealed in Acts 1:8. Jesus says, *Ye shall receive power, when the Holy Spirit is come upon you: and ye shall be my witnesses both in Jerusalem, and in all Judaea and Samaria, and unto the uttermost part of the earth.* The baptism with the Holy Spirit, the gift of the Holy Spirit, is given to you and me to make us effective in God's service.

Many of you pray for the baptism with the Holy Spirit day after day, week after week, month after month, year after year, and get nothing. Why? Because you are seeking a blessing that terminates in yourself. You are seeking God's blessing but not seeking it for God's purpose. When you are ready to go out and tell others about Christ as best you can in God's power, when you are willing to go out and plead with men, women, and children to accept the Lord Jesus Christ, then and only then can you have the gift of the Holy Spirit.

> Some are seeking God's blessing but not seeking it for God's purpose.

For the Most Charitable Results

In the fifth place, soul winning should be the business of every one of us because it produces the most benevolent results. No other work is as beneficial; no other work is comparable to the work of bringing other men and women to a saving knowledge of Jesus Christ. To feed the hungry, to clothe the naked, to house the poor, and to instruct the ignorant is blessed work, and I rejoice in all the work of that kind that is being done. But to clothe the naked, feed the hungry, house the poor, and instruct the ignorant is not to be compared with the glory, honor, and goodness of bringing lost people to a saving knowledge of Jesus Christ. There is no work like it.

There is one passage in this Book which, if I could repeat

that passage to bring out the full meaning and force of three words, I would be willing to leave here without preaching another sermon. If I could quote that passage as it ought to be quoted to make you realize the full, entire meaning and force of three specific words, you would rise *en masse* and go out at the close of this meeting. You would go up and down the streets for days, and weeks, and months, and years to come, begging men and women to be reconciled to God.

You say, "What is this passage?"

It is a very familiar one. You all know it, but you know the words so well you have never stopped to consider the meaning. It is James 5:20: *Let him know, that he who converteth a sinner from the error of his way shall save a soul from death.* I would to God that I could burn these words into your hearts today – *he who converteth a sinner from the error of his way shall save a soul from death.* The three words to note and consider are *save, soul,* and *death.*

Let us begin with the middle word – *soul. Shall save a soul from death.* If I only had power to make you see the value of a soul as God sees it, not merely the value of the soul of the philosopher, the highly educated man, or the prince or the nobleman. If only you could see the value of the soul of the drunkard, the outcast woman, the uneducated man, the igno-ramus, or of the little, ragged, dirty boy or girl upon the street. If only I could make you see and feel the value of one soul as God sees it! What can I put in comparison with that? Gold is nothing in comparison with the value of a soul. Precious stones are nothing; all the gems of earth are as nothing.

In 1893, during the World's Fair in Chicago, I could never get close enough to see what the people were looking at in the Tiffany Exhibit in the Manufactures Building. Time and again and day after day I went to that place, at all hours of the day and night, but there was always such a crowd there that if I wanted to see what they were looking at, I had to stand on my tiptoes and look over the heads of the crowd in front of me. What were they looking at? Nothing but a cone of purple velvet revolving upon its axis; toward its apex was a large, beautiful diamond of fabulous value. Day after day people by the thousands came to see it, and during the course of the World's Fair, literally a million people came to look at that one stone. Well, it was worth looking at, but I have never thought much of that sight since.

But it has occurred to me that the soul of one man or woman, the soul of the drunkard on the street, the soul of the vilest abandoned woman, or the soul of the filthiest, most ignorant boy or girl upon the street is of infinitely more value in God's sight than ten thousand diamonds like that.

I had two friends in New York City in the same business, and both of them prospered. One of these men started in New York City practically penniless, but he had a rare business ability. He succeeded in amassing a fortune of first a million dollars, then two million dollars, then three million dollars, and then four million dollars. One day he was walking toward his beautiful home up on Fifth Avenue, and as he crossed one of the lower avenues of the city, he was run into by a streetcar and taken home to die. He left four million dollars. Yes, he left it all. He did not take a penny of it with him. And I remember how the New York and the Brooklyn papers came out with editorials upon this self-made man, speaking of his remarkable business ability. He had come to New York as a young man without any money, had gone to work and amassed a fortune of four million dollars, and then died.

The other man was in the same business. He too had prospered, though I don't know just how much he accumulated; I think about half a million dollars. Then one day God came into that man's home and took a beautiful daughter, a child only four years old, the idol of that man's heart. A few days after her burial, he was riding in the elevated train toward his home, and as he thought of his little daughter, blinding tears came to his eyes. He held the newspaper in front of his face to hide the tears from the strangers in the train. He kept thinking about his little daughter Florence, and this question came into his heart – "Your daughter is dead; what are you doing for other men's daughters?"

He said, "I am doing nothing, but I will." The next year he put ten thousand dollars into the rescue of fallen girls in New York City; the following year he put eleven thousand dollars into the same work; and the year after that he put himself into the work. He turned his back on his place of business down on Fulton Street, often going to his place of business for only two hours a week and spending eighteen or twenty hours a day in the slums of New York City, seeking the perishing. Finally, he turned his back on the business altogether, sold it for a profit, and gave his whole time and strength to telling the lost about Jesus Christ.

He is nearly seventy years old – the youngest seventy-year-old man I know. God has used him to lift thousands from the deepest depths of sin to a saving knowledge of Jesus Christ.

Now, I am going to ask you a question. In light of eternity and that great judgment day to which we are all hurrying, which of these two men made the best use of his time, his talents, and his money? Did the man who devoted his entire energies to saving four million dollars, leaving it all when he died as a pauper, do better than the man who devoted his strength to saving thousands of souls who will meet and welcome him in a glorious eternity?

The second word is *death. Shall save a soul from death.* That word *death* is one of the worst words in our language. People in our day, poets and theologians, try to paint death in fair colors. There is nothing fair about death. Death is a hideous thing; death is a horrid thing; death is an appalling thing; and death is our enemy. Thank God, for the Christian death is a conquered enemy, for Jesus Christ has abolished death and brought life and immortality to light through the gospel. But death itself is an appalling thing.

When you go to a man, woman, or child and lead them to a saving knowledge of Jesus Christ, you have saved a soul from death. Remember, the death of the soul does not mean mere nonexistence; death does not mean annihilation; death does not mean mere cessation of being. Death does not mean mere nonexistence any more than life in the New Testament means mere existence.

> Thank God, for the Christian death is a conquered enemy.

Life means right existence, holy existence, godlike existence, the ennoblement, glorification, and deification of existence; death means just the opposite. Death means wrong existence, unholy existence; it means corruption, defilement, degradation, shame, disgrace, ruin, and the despair of existence. When you and I lead a man or woman to Christ, we save a soul from death.

Then look at that other word – *save*. That is one of the great words. You sometimes narrow it down and make it a very small sort of word, but as it is used in the Bible, the word *save* is one of the most magnificent words. It means not merely to save *from*, but also to save *to*, not merely to save from hell, but also to save to glory, holiness, happiness, heaven, and knowledge of God, communion with God, and likeness to God.

Suppose it were announced that I would go tell the businessmen in this city this afternoon about a process whereby they could go out through the streets into your country roads, stoop down in the mud and dirt, pick up common ordinary stones, and by the mysterious process of the jeweler, transform them into real diamonds of the very first quality. Suppose it had been announced that I would do that today and that the businessmen knew I really had such a process. Do you think there would have been anybody in this meeting this afternoon? There would not have been seats enough to accommodate the crowd of men that would have come.

I can tell you that very thing. I can tell you how to go out through the streets and into your country roads, stoop down into the mud and dirt and mire of sin, pick out the common, ordinary, rude stones of lost souls, and by the glorious art of the soul winner, transform them into diamonds worthy of a place in the Savior's eternal diadem. Don't you think that is worthwhile? Is anything else worth as much?

Most Abundant Reward

And last, soul winning should be the business of every Christian because it brings the most-abundant reward. There is another verse which I wish to sink into your heart. It is Daniel 12:3: *They that be wise shall shine as the brightness of the firmament; and they that turn many to righteousness as the stars for ever and ever.* Some people want to shine on earth. It is not worthwhile. The brightest star in any earthly galaxy will soon fade. The brightest star in the financial firmament, the brightest star in the political firmament, or the brightest star in the social firmament – how long will they shine? Only a few years, and then they will go out forever.

Three years ago the brightest star in our political firmament shone with unrivaled splendor. He was a man about whom the world was speaking and beginning to associate his name with the names of America's greatest statesmen – Washington and Lincoln, but one dark night that star was snuffed out by the crack of the revolver of a half-crazy anarchist. Today that great statesman is practically forgotten. Almost no one ever speaks about McKinley today. You can look through our papers day after day and never see his name. It is all Roosevelt now; it used to be all McKinley. Ten years from now it will all be somebody else.

It is the same in England. You go through your English papers today. It is all Chamberlain now. Ten years from now, Chamberlain will be practically forgotten. It doesn't pay to shine down here. It does pay to shine up there. They that shine up there shall shine as the stars forever and ever. Most of us could not shine down here if we wanted to, but thank God, any of us can shine up there. There is only one way to shine up there, and that is by saving the lost, by bringing them to a saving knowledge of Christ.

Before I close, I must tell you a story. This incident is so remarkable that when I first heard it, I thought that it could not possibly be true. Yet the man who told it was of such a character that I felt that it must be true. Yet I said, "I must find out for myself whether that story is true or not." So I went to the librarian of the university where the incident was said to have occurred, and I found out that it was true. The story as I tell you today is as I got it from the brother of the main character in the incident. The incident is this:

About twelve miles from where I live, twelve miles from the city of Chicago, is the suburb of Evanston, where there is a large Methodist university, probably the largest university of the Methodist denomination in America. Years ago, before the college had blossomed into a great university, there were many students, and among them were two young country boys from the state of Iowa. They were strong, vigorous fellows, and one of them was a famous swimmer. Early one morning word came to the college that down on Lake Michigan off the shores of Evanston, there was a wreck. It proved to be the *Lady Elgin*.

The college boys hurried down to the shores of Lake Michigan along with everybody in town. Far in the distance, they saw the *Lady Elgin* breaking into pieces. Ed Spencer, this famous swimmer, threw off all his superfluous garments, tied a rope around his waist, threw one end to his comrades on the shore, and dove into Lake Michigan. He swam out to the wreck, grasped one person that was drowning, and gave the sign to be pulled ashore. Again, and again, and again he swam out and grasped a drowning man or woman and brought them safely to shore, until he had brought a seventh, an eighth, a ninth, and a tenth. Then he was utterly exhausted.

They had built a fire of logs upon the sand, so he stood by the fire that cold, bleak morning; he was blue, pinched, trembling, and hardly able to stand. He stood before that fire, trying to get a little warmth into his perishing limbs. As he stood there, he turned and looked at Lake Michigan, and off in the distance, near the *Lady Elgin,* he saw men and women still struggling in the water. He said, "Boys, I am going in again."

"No, no, Ed," they cried, "it is futile to try; you have used up all your strength; you could not save anybody; for you to jump into the lake will simply mean for you to commit suicide."

"Well, boys," he said, "they are drowning, and I will try anyhow." And he started to the shore of the lake.

His companions cried, "No, no, Ed, no, don't try."

He said, "I will," and he jumped into Lake Michigan and battled out against the waves. He grabbed a drowning man that was struggling in the water. Again, and again, and again he went out, until he had brought an eleventh, a twelfth, a thirteenth, a fourteenth, and a fifteenth person safely to shore. Then they pulled him in through the breakers. He could scarcely get to the fire on the beach, and there he stood trembling before that fire, trying to get a little warmth into his shivering limbs.

As they looked at him, it seemed as if the hand of death were already upon him.

Then he turned away from the fire again, looked over the lake, and as he looked, far in the distance he saw a spar[5] rising and falling upon the waves. He looked at it with his keen eye and saw a man's head above the spar. He said, "Boys, there's a man trying to save himself." He looked again and saw a woman's head beside the man's. He said, "Boys, there's a man trying to save his wife." He watched the spar as it drifted toward the point. He knew that to drift around that point meant certain death. He said, "Boys, I am going to help him."

"No, no, Ed," they cried, "you can't help him. Your strength is all gone."

He said, "I will try anyway." He dove into Lake Michigan and swam out wearily toward the spar; as he reached it, he put his hands on the spar, summoned all his dying strength, and brought that spar around the right end of the point to safety. Then they pulled him in through the breakers, and loving hands lifted him from the beach and carried him to his room at the college. They laid him upon his bed and made a fire in the grate; his brother Will stayed to watch him, for he was becoming delirious.

As the day passed, Will Spencer sat by the fire. Suddenly Will heard a gentle footfall behind him and felt someone touch him on the back; he looked up, and there stood Ed, looking wistfully down into his face. He said, "What is it, Ed?"

He said, "Will, did I do my best?"

"Why, Ed," he said, "you saved seventeen."

He said, "I know that, but I was afraid I didn't do my very best. Will, do you think I did my very best?"

Will took him back to bed and laid him on it; he sat down by his side. As the night passed, Ed went into semi-delirium,

---

5   A stout pole used for masts on a ship.

and Will sat by the bed, held his hand, and tried to calm him. All that he thought about were the men and women that perished that day, for in spite of all his bravery, many went down to a watery grave.

Will tried to calm him. "Ed," he said, "you saved seventeen."

He said, "I know it, Will, I know it; but oh, if I could have only saved just one more."

You and I stand beside a stormy sea. As we look out at this tossing sea of life around us on every side, there are wrecks. Will you and I sit calmly while they are going down, down, down, down to a hopeless eternity?

Let us plunge in again and again, until every last ounce of strength is gone, and when at last in sheer exhaustion we fall on the shore in the earnestness of our love for perishing men, let us cry, "Oh, if I could only save just one more."

Chapter 16

The Most Effective Method of Soul Winning

He findeth first his own brother Simon, and . . .
He brought him unto Jesus. (John 1:41-42)

The one who brought his brother to Jesus in this passage was Andrew. We are not told that Andrew ever preached a sermon in his life. If he did, the Holy Spirit did not think it was worth putting on record; but this brother, whom he brought to Jesus, preached a sermon that led three thousand people to Jesus in one day. Where would Simon Peter's sermon have been if it had not been for Andrew's personal work?

The most important kind of Christian work in the world is personal work. We look at the men who stand on the platform and speak to great crowds, but I believe God pays more attention to the man who sits down with a single soul.

A blind woman once came to my office in Chicago and said, "You don't think my blindness will keep me from doing Christian work, do you?"

"No," I replied. "On the contrary, I think it might be a great help to you. A great many people, seeing your blindness, will come and sit down with you, and you can talk with them about the Savior."

"That is not what I mean. I don't want to talk to one person. When a woman can talk to five hundred or six hundred, she doesn't want to spend time talking to one."

I said to her, "Your Master could talk to five thousand at once, for we have it on record, and He did not think it beneath His dignity to talk to one at a time."

Have you ever thought of the tremendous power that there is in personal face-to-face work? One day a man in Boston had a boy fresh from the country in his Sunday school class. He was an uneducated boy, and he knew almost nothing about the Bible. He did not even know where to look to find the Gospel of John. He was embarrassed because the other boys were educated boys and knew their Bibles.

> Have you ever thought of the tremendous power that there is in personal face-to-face work?

He was just a green country boy, seventeen years old, but that Sunday school teacher had a heart full of love for Christ and perishing souls. So one day he went to the boot shop where that boy worked and said, "Wouldn't you like to be a Christian?"

The boy had never been approached that way before. Nobody had ever spoken to him about his soul. He said, "Yes, I would like to be a Christian."

And that Sunday school teacher explained what it meant to be a Christian, and then he said, "Let us pray." They knelt down in the back of that boot shop, and the boy, as far as he knew, became a Christian. That boy was Dwight L. Moody. If it had not been for Edward Kimball's faithful, personal work, where would Dwight L. Moody and his great work throughout the world have been?

Some Sunday school teachers probably say, "I wish I could get to the great meeting in the big hall, but I have to stay here just teaching a lot of little boys and girls." Who knows who is in that little class of yours? Who knows what your little, ignorant, ragged boy may become? All you teachers, make up your mind; by God's help, you can make an honest effort to lead everybody in your Sunday school class to Christ today. This world will never be saved by preaching in churches alone, but this world could soon be evangelized by personal work.

Suppose there are two thousand people here, and suppose every one of you became a personal worker. Then suppose, by your very best effort, you only succeeded in leading one person to Christ in a year, and that one led one to Christ the next year, and so on; what would be the result? At the end of the first year there would be four thousand; at the end of two years there would be eight thousand; at the end of three years sixteen thousand; at the end of four years thirty-two thousand. If this continued for eight years, your whole city would be won for Christ. At the end of thirty-five years, every man, woman, and child on the face of the earth would have heard the gospel. There is not one person who cannot lead at least one other one to Christ this year. You can instruct everyone that you lead to Christ to go out and be a soul winner. After you reach them and they are converted, send them out to lead others by bringing in another; you will soon touch the whole city.

Advantages of Personal Work

Anyone
The first advantage is that anyone can do it. You cannot all preach. I am glad you can't. What an institution this world would be if we were all preachers! You cannot all sing like Alexander. I am glad you can't, for if you could, he would be no curiosity, and

you would not come out to hear him sing and give me a chance to preach to you. You can't all even teach Sunday school classes. Some people have an idea that any converted person can teach a Sunday school class. I don't believe it. I think we are making a great mistake in this respect, in allowing unqualified persons to teach in Sunday schools. But there is not a child of God who cannot do personal work. A mother with a large family knows she is not called to be a preacher, but she can do personal work better than anybody else.

A lady who had five children came to me one time and said (I think she had been reading the life of Frances Willard), "I wish I could do some work like that for Christ."

I said, "You can work for Christ among all the people you move among." I watched that woman. Every one of her children was brought to Christ – every one! Every maid that came to work in that home was dealt with about her soul. Every butcher's boy or grocer's boy that came around to the door was dealt with about his soul. Every time she went out shopping, she made it a point to talk with the man or woman behind the counter. And when, one dark day, death came into that home and took away a sweet little child, she did not forget to speak to the undertaker, who came to do the last offices for the dead, about his soul. He told me that nothing had ever impressed him in his life as that woman had when in the midst of her sorrow, she was interested in his soul.

An invalid can do personal work. I have a friend in New York City who has left a life of wealth and fashion to go to work among the outcast. One day she reached a poor outcast girl. She did not live much more than a year after that lady had led her to Christ. She took her to her home to die. As Delia was dying, she wrote to her friends – some in Sing Sing Prison, some in the Tombs of New York City. All her friends were among the criminal class. She told them about Christ. She invited those who were not behind prison bars to come and see her. My friend told me, "There was a constant procession up the stairway of outcast women and men who came to see Delia, and I knew of one hundred of the most hopeless people in New York City that she led to Christ before she died." That puts us to shame! Suppose God kindled a fire right here in your hearts, and you received the anointing of the Spirit of Christ; every one of you would start to do personal work. You would not need any evangelist to come from abroad. That is what we have come for – to stir you up to do it.

Anywhere

The second advantage is that you can do it in any place. You cannot preach in every place. You can preach in the churches two or three times a week; you can preach in the town hall occasionally; and you can preach in the streets sometimes. But you cannot go into the factories and preach often or hold services, but you can go there and do personal work, if you hire on there. One man came to our meetings in Liverpool from Hudson's Dry Soap factory, and he was converted. Every once in awhile, I get a letter telling me of their meetings, and now they have a meeting that they conduct outside the building somewhere. In Bradley's foundry a workman got a card for the meetings, but he could not go. He handed it over to the wickedest man in the shop. That man was grateful for the invitation and wanted to show his appreciation by going. He was converted at the very first meeting and went back and told his companions, which created a revival in the foundry.

A telegraph messenger boy was converted in Manchester, and before we finished our services there, seventy messenger boys were converted in Manchester. There is not a hotel, or a factory, or a tavern where you cannot do personal work.

Any Time

The third advantage is that you can do it at any time – any hour of the night, 365 days in the year. Certainly, you cannot preach every hour of the day. If you preach three times a day, you are doing well, but there is not an hour of the day or night, between midnight one night and midnight the next night, that you cannot do personal work. You can go out on the streets at night and find the poor wanderers. When I lived in Minneapolis, I employed a missionary just to go out on the streets at night, to speak to the drunkards, outcast women, and night workers, and some of the best conversions were among these people. This missionary had been an outcast herself at one time and was leading them to the Christ that she had found.

Soon after Mr. Moody was converted, he made up his mind that he would not let a day go by without speaking to someone about their soul. One night he came home late – it was nearly ten o'clock. He said, "Here, I haven't spoken to my man today. I guess I have lost my chance." He saw a man standing under the lamppost and said to himself, "There's my last chance." He hurried up to him and said, "Are you a Christian?"

"It's none of your business, and if you were not some sort of preacher, I would knock you into the gutter."

"Well," Mr. Moody said, "I just wanted to lead you to Christ."

The next day that man went to a friend of Mr. Moody's and said, "That man Moody has got zeal without knowledge. He spoke to me in the street last night and asked me if I was a Christian. It is none of his business. If he had not been some sort of preacher, I would have knocked him down. He has zeal without knowledge. He is doing more harm than good."

This friend of Mr. Moody's came to him and said, "See here, Moody, it's all right to be passionate, but you have zeal without knowledge. You are doing more harm than good." (Let me say here, it is better to have zeal without knowledge than knowledge without zeal.)

Mr. Moody went out, feeling rather cheap and crestfallen. A few weeks passed, and one night there was an awful pounding at his door. Mr. Moody got up and opened the door, and there was this very man.

He said, "Mr. Moody, I haven't had a night's peace since you spoke to me that night under the lamppost. I've come to ask you to show me how to be a Christian." Mr. Moody took him in and showed him the way of life. And when the Civil War broke out, that man went and laid down his life for his country.

Another time the thought came to Mr. Moody after he was in bed: "You have not spoken to your man today." But he said, "I am in bed. I cannot get up and go out now." But he could not rest, so he got up and went and opened the door, and it was pouring rain. "Well," he said, "there is no use going out on the street this awful night. There won't be a soul out in this pouring rain." Just then he heard the patter of a man's feet and saw a man coming. As he came up, Mr. Moody rushed out and said, "Can I have the shelter of your umbrella?"

> A great many people cannot be reached in any other way than by personal work.

"Certainly."

"Have you got a shelter in the time of storm?" he asked him, and he pointed him to Jesus.

Any Class of People

The fourth advantage is that it reaches all classes. A great many people cannot be reached in any other way than by personal work. Thousands of people could not come to church if they would, and thousands would not come to church if they could. This is a splendid hall, adapted for our purpose, and it will hold about 10,000 women this afternoon and 10,000 men tonight; that is 20,000 people inside, and there will be 580,000 outside. It is the 580,000 that we are after. You cannot reach them through the church; you cannot reach them at the open-air meeting; you cannot reach them in rescue missions. There is only one way you can reach them, and that is by personal work. There is not a man, woman, or child that you cannot reach by personal work. You can reach the policemen, the streetcar men, the railway men; there is no one that you cannot reach by personal work.

Specific Targets

The fifth advantage is that it hits the mark. In preaching you have to be more or less general. In personal work, you have just one man, or just one woman, to talk to, and you can hit the mark every time. You have heard of Henry Ward Beecher. He went out shooting with his father one day. He had often gone before, but he had never shot anything in his life. Way down yonder was a squirrel. His father said, "Henry, do you see that squirrel?"

"Yes, Father."

"Would you like to hit it?"

"Yes, Father; but I never hit anything in my life."

"You lay the barrel of your gun across the top rail down here, and look right down along the barrel. Henry, do you see the squirrel?"

"Yes, Father."

"Well, pull the trigger."

He pulled the trigger, and the squirrel fell at the first shot. The first thing he ever shot in his life. Why? Because it was the first thing he had ever aimed at.

That is the trouble with a good deal of our preaching; we aim at nothing and hit it every time. This is the advantage of personal work; we aim at one definite person.

But in our preaching, as Mr. Moody used to say, "I speak to

this lady on the front seat, and she applies it to the man behind her; he applies it to the woman behind him, and she applies it to the man behind her, and they keep applying it until they apply it out the back door. We have a wonderful power of applying the good points of a sermon to somebody else. When it comes to personal work, there is nobody else to apply it to. I try to be personal in my preaching; be just as personal as you can, and you may still miss your mark.

A man came to my church one morning, excessively pious, not having an anointing of the Holy Spirit, but pious. This man always talked about "the deeper life" but didn't have an ordinary, decent, everyday kind of Christian life. He had all the phraseology of the deepest Christian experience; he talked about being filled with the Spirit, but at the same time cheated other people in business. I saw him come into the audience, and I said to myself, "I am glad you have come. I will hit you this morning. I have a sermon just for you." While I was preaching, I would look right at him, so he would know I meant him; he sat there, beaming up at me, and when the sermon was over, he came to me rubbing his hands.

"Oh," he said, "Brother Torrey, I came eight miles to hear you this morning. I have so enjoyed it."

That was just what I did not want. I wanted to make him miserable. But I had him now face-to-face, and he did not enjoy it. That is the advantage of personal work. You can aim right square at the mark and hit it. A man can stand preaching all day, but he will say, "I don't like this personal work." It hits too hard. You don't like to have a person come up and say, "Are you a Christian?" The minister can preach all he pleases, but when he looks you right in the eye, you know he means you. The message aims right straight at the mark and hits it.

Effectiveness

The sixth advantage is that it is effective. Personal work succeeds where every other kind of work fails. I don't care who the preacher is or how good a preacher may be; a man or woman who has not been affected by the sermon will be reached by some very ordinary person with the love of God and the love of souls in his heart. Take Mr. Moody, for example. I think Mr. Moody was as good a preacher as I ever heard. I would rather hear Mr. Moody preach a sermon that I had heard a dozen times than to hear any other man preach a sermon I had never heard at all. But as good a preacher as Mr. Moody was, thousands of people would leave utterly unmoved by his sermons. I have seen very ordinary working people, uneducated people, but people who had the love of Christ and the love of souls in their heart, connect with the man or woman who had left Mr. Moody's meeting, and in ten or fifteen minutes lead them to the Lord Jesus Christ.

Specific Needs

The seventh advantage is that it meets the specific need and every need of the individual. Even when a man comes to Christ, he has difficulties and doubts, troubles and questions. He cannot ask them of the preacher. How often a man sits down in the audience and says, "I wish I could speak to that preacher alone." In this personal, face-to-face work, a man can ask all the questions he wants, and you can meet all his difficulties. I get letters from people all over the world who have difficulties.

My father used to tell a story (he did not vouch for its truth), but he reported that there was a physician in the village who had a jug, and he took a little of every kind of medicine he had in his shop and put it in that jug and shook it up. When people came to him and he did not know just what their problem was, he would give them a spoonful out of that jug, thinking, "There is something in it that will meet their disorder anyhow."

That is what we do in our preaching; we take a little comfort and put it in the sermon – a little bit of conviction, a little bit to show the way of life. We shake it all up and give it to the people. If I were going to be doctored, I would want the doctor to find out my specific difficulty, and I would want to take the kind of medicine that met my specific need. In personal work, you give specific passages of Scripture for specific difficulties.

Abundant Results
The eighth advantage is that it produces abundant results. The great services where the ministers speak to five hundred, or a thousand, or five thousand do not produce as abundant results. Suppose a man was pastor of a church of a hundred members, and suppose he was a very faithful minister. As a result of his preaching, fifty were added to his church each year on confession of faith. That would be a good record. In the report of the Presbyterian churches of America, only two hundred of the seven thousand reported over fifty additions for the year. But suppose by his faithful preaching, this pastor added fifty a year. Now suppose that pastor said, "I am going to train my people to do personal work." Suppose he trained his people, and suppose only one-half of them would consent to do it. If these fifty trained workers each succeeded in winning one person a month to Christ, that would mean six hundred a year. Preaching is not in it with personal work.

But some of us think we pay the minister to do the work. You don't do anything of the kind. Your minister is your leader, and you are supposed to work under his leadership. One reason the church of which I am pastor always has a revival is

> In personal work, you give specific passages of Scripture for specific difficulties.

that the people are trained to do personal work. It has had a revival ever since I have been pastor there. I have been pastor for ten years. There have been ten years of revival. There has never been a month that we have not received new members. There has never been a Sunday without conversions. We would not know what to make of it if there were a Sunday without conversions. I do not think there has been any day in the week of all this time – 3,650 days in all – that someone has not been won to Christ in or around the building. There will be a good many people converted there today. You say, "Who is going to preach?" I don't know. But whoever preaches, there will be conversions, and in the Sunday school this afternoon there will be conversions, and in the evening meeting tonight there will be conversions. Why? Because I have a church that believes in and does personal work.

Every Sunday evening while I preach, I know there is someone near everyone in that church who knows how to lead a soul to Christ. There are workers in every section of the church. If anybody gets up and goes out, I know that there is at least one person that is going to be spoken to that night. I like it in Chicago, because just as sure as anybody gets up and leaves, someone will drop down the stairs behind them and perhaps follow them a block or two before they speak to them.

Go out to the people and ask God to give you power. The Holy Spirit is for every one of us. I thank God that the great gift of the Son is for the whole world and that the gift of the Holy Spirit is for every saved one. *If ye then, being evil, know how to give good gifts unto your children, how much more shall your heavenly Father give the Holy Spirit to them that ask him?* (Luke 11:13). Just ask, and then go out. Of course, you need to know something about your Bible in order to do personal work, but you only need one text to start with.

When Mr. Moody first came to New Haven, we thought we

would go out and hear this strange, uneducated man. I was in the senior class in the theological department of the university and was just about to get my B.Div. degree. I knew more then than I will ever know in my life again. We thought we would patronize Mr. Moody a little bit. He did not seem at all honored by our presence, and as we heard that untutored man, we thought, "He may be uneducated, but he knows some things we don't." Some of us had sense enough to go to him and say, "Mr. Moody, we wish you would tell us how to do it."

If you never start until you are sure you will not make a blunder, you will make the biggest blunder of your life.

And he told us to come around early the next night, and he would tell us. So we theologues went up to the meeting, and he said a few words to us, gave us a few texts of Scripture, and then said, "You go at it." The best way to learn how to do it is to do it.

He that goeth forth and weepeth, bearing seed for sowing, shall doubtless come again with joy, bringing his sheaves with him (Psalm 126:6). If, however, you make a stupid blunder the first time, go at it again. But if you never start until you are sure you will not make a blunder, you will make the biggest blunder of your life. Go alone with God first, and see if you are right with God; put away every known sin in your life; surrender absolutely to God; ask for the Holy Spirit; and then pitch in.

Chapter 17

Simple Methods by Which Anyone Can Win Others to Christ

And the Spirit said unto Philip, Go near, and join
thyself to this chariot. And Philip ran to him,
and heard him reading Isaiah the prophet, and
said, Understandest thou what thou readest?
(Acts 8:29-30)

One of the greatest joys on earth is the joy of bringing others to a saving knowledge of Christ. I have heard people say that when they were converted, the whole world seemed different; the sun seemed to shine with a new light; there was new music in the song of the birds; and all nature seemed clothed with new beauty and glory. I had no such experience when I was converted. In fact, I was converted in the middle of the night, and the sun was not shining at all. But I did have such an experience the first time that I led another one to a definite acceptance of Jesus Christ as their definite Savior.

I had been dealing with this person for two solid hours and seemed to be making little headway; then at the very close, he yielded and accepted Christ. When I left the building where this decision had been made, it was nearly sunset in the springtime; the whole world seemed to have a beauty that I had never seen before. I felt like I was walking on air; my heart was filled with joy such as I had never known. No other joy compares to the joy of saving men, and it is possible for every child of God, no matter how humble and ungifted, to have this joy.

God's most approved method of winning others to Christ is indicated in the text: the method of personal, face-to-face dealing with the lost. The high estimate that God places upon this form of work is seen in the context. Philip was in the midst of a great revival in Samaria; great crowds assembled daily to listen, and a strange command came to him to leave this great work that had stirred the whole city and go to the way that went *from Jerusalem unto Gaza: the same is desert* (Acts 8:26). Wise man as he was, strange as the order must have seemed, Philip, without a moment's questioning or hesitation, *arose and went.* An inquiring soul passed by in his chariot, and the Spirit of God whispered to Philip, *Go near, and join thyself to this chariot,* and *Philip ran.* If only we were as prompt to obey the first whisper of the Spirit when He bids us to go and speak to others. Our Master did not consider it beneath Himself to speak to one at a time. We have more frequent records of His dealing with individuals than we have of His preaching sermons to vast audiences. The one-by-one method of soul winning is the method that God delights to honor. But how shall we do it?

Select Your Man to Win

In personal work, as in all forms of work, specificity is of tremendous importance. There are hosts of people who have a longing to win someone to Christ, but they do not pick out any specific individual to win, so they fail. A precise purpose to lead some specific individual to a distinct acceptance of a specific Savior will accomplish vastly more than a vague longing to lead an indefinite number of indefinite persons into some ambiguous experience. But how shall we select the individuals whom we are to win to Christ?

Try Prayer

Some persons are the peculiar property of each of us. We can lead them to Christ, and no one else can. Who these persons are God alone knows, but He is willing to tell us if we will only ask Him. We should go to Him and ask Him to show us who the persons are that He would have us lead to Christ. Then we should wait on Him, listen for His voice – that still, small voice – as it speaks in our hearts. When He mentions that person, we should write that one's name down and determine that we will lead that person to Christ.

> We should go to God and ask Him to show us who the persons are that He would have us lead to Christ.

Select Those Who Are Accessible

The most accessible of all are those in our own family, and that is the place to begin – in your own home. Jesus said to the demoniac whom He had healed and who wished to accompany Him on His missionary journeys, *Return to thy house, and declare how great things God hath done for thee* (Luke 8:39). When Andrew found Christ, he went *first [to] his own brother Simon, and . . . brought him unto Jesus* (John 1:41-42). No one of us should rest as long as any member of our own household is unsaved. I do not mean that we should confine our efforts to them, but we should begin with them and keep after them. Some say that the hardest persons to lead to Christ are those in our own households. This is not true. If your life is right with God, no one will know it as well as those who live with you, and no one else can influence them as well as you can. The holiest and sweetest privilege that a father or mother has is the privilege of bringing their own children to Christ.

We are commanded to do this in the Word of God: *And, ye fathers, provoke not your children to wrath: but nurture them in the chastening and admonition of the Lord* (Ephesians 6:4). And this we can do, for God does not command the impossible. I should feel that my wife and I had been robbed of one of the sweetest privileges of life if anyone else should lead one of our children to Christ. Of course, I would infinitely rather they would be led by someone else to Christ than not to be led at all, but it is our sacred privilege to do it ourselves.

Next to those in your own family are those with whom you are associated in business or in work. If you are a shop assistant, go to work on your own coworkers; if you are a laboring man, go to work on your fellow laborers; if you are a businessman, go to work on your partners and your employees; if you are a student, go to work on your fellow students. Try first for the man next to you.

I meet many people who desire to win men to Christ in China, but they are not willing to make any strong effort to win to Christ the unsaved members in their own homes or their next-door neighbors. Sending anyone out as a foreign missionary who has not first demonstrated their love for souls and their capacity to win them to Christ by winning others to Christ at home is a suicidal policy.

Select Those Who Are Approachable

As a rule, those of your age are more approachable than those of a widely different age. Young men are best to deal with young men, middle-aged men with middle-aged men, and old men with old men. Children often have more influence with children than adults do.

Select those of the same sex. As a rule, it is best for men to deal with men, and women to deal with women. That rule has a few exceptions, but not many. Immense mischief has come through the disregard of this rule of practical wisdom. I always take it as a bad sign when I see young men who are constantly dealing with young women, or young women who are constantly dealing with young men. I have never known a case of this kind that did not turn out badly. Some of the saddest tragedies I have ever known have come through mistakes of this sort. Of course, an elderly, motherly woman can deal wisely with young men and boys, and occasionally elderly men can deal wisely with little girls and young women, but my long experience with Christian workers has strengthened the conviction in me of the wisdom of the rule: men with men, and women with women.

Select people of the same station in life. This rule also has exceptions. There are notable instances on record where servants have led their masters to Christ. (The great Earl of Shaftesbury was led to Christ by a nurse in the home.) But as a rule, people can be most readily approached by others in the same class of society. No one can deal as well with a lawyer as another lawyer; no one can deal as well with a physician as another physician; no one, as a rule, can deal as well with a tradesman as another tradesman; no one can deal as effectively with a student as a fellow student.

Select those who are agreeable. To all of us some people are pleasant and others are not. Just why they are agreeable, we cannot always tell, but we know it is a fact. Some who take to Alexander do not take to me, and some who take to me do not take to Alexander. Now those who take to me are the ones for me to deal with, and those who take to Alexander are the people for Alexander to deal with. Alexander can reach people that I could not touch, but I can reach people that Alexander cannot touch.

However we may account for these things, they are facts, and a wise soul winner always takes account of facts. He concerns himself more with facts than with the philosophy of the facts; he acts upon the facts and lets the philosophy of them take care of itself. There is not a person who doesn't have some acquaintance that he can touch and that nobody else in the world can touch. You are responsible before God for that one. You need not confine yourself absolutely to those whom you select to win; always be ready at the slightest opening of opportunity to win anyone to Christ that comes your way. But concentrate on the one you do select. Never lose sight of the fact that you are to win that man for Christ, and never rest until he is won.

> Never lose sight of the fact that you are to win "that man" for Christ, and never rest until he is won.

Lay Siege for Him

When you have selected your man to win, the next thing is to lay siege for him. Do you know what it is to lay siege for a soul? Did you ever select a certain individual and lay siege for that individual to win him to Christ, cost what it may and take as long as it might? You know how an insurance agent conducts his business. He goes into a town and selects those who seem to be likely risks; then he lays siege for them. He writes them letters; he sends them literature; he calls upon them; he persistently follows up on them; he studies them. He learns their tastes and how they can be best approached, and he never rests until he has insured these persons that he has selected to insure.

I have had some experience with the persistent attentions of these insurance agents. I have nothing to say against their determination; I simply want to recommend their methods to soul winners. Shouldn't we be as businesslike and as much in earnest in insuring people for eternity as an insurance agent is in insuring them for time? He does it for the money that he can make out of it; we do it for a higher objective – the glory of God and the salvation of those whom we are pursuing. But how shall we lay siege for them?

By prayer

When you have selected a man to win for Christ, you should pursue him by prayer day and night, day after day, week after week, and if need be, year after year. In order to be specific, make a prayer list. Write on a sheet of paper: "God helping me, I promise to pray earnestly and work persistently for the salvation of the following persons." Then kneel down and ask God to tell you who to put on that list. Do not make it too long. When you have made it, keep your promise. One by one as they accept Christ, you can take their names off the list and add others. Everywhere we have gone around the world, we have had people make such prayer lists as this, and people are constantly coming to us and telling us, "Another one gone off my prayer list."

One of the leading businessmen of Belfast, an active Christian worker, made such a prayer list when we were in that city. He came to me toward the close of the mission and said, "The last one has gone off my prayer list today. They have all been saved."

By personal effort

It is well to pray, but it is not enough to pray. Praying for the salvation of others is an act of insincerity unless we are willing to go to those for whom we pray and talk with them; beg them to be reconciled to God. Sometimes you will not go for the conquest of the soul directly; you will first prepare the way.

Last season, while I was holding missions around the country, my family resided in Southport. I would go there to spend my holidays. The first time I went there, I met a man whom God laid upon my heart and whom I determined to win for Christ. He was a most unlikely case. He had once been in a good position but had plummeted with alcohol. I cultivated his acquaintance, gained his friendship, and watched for my opportunity to win him for Christ. Every time I met him on the street, I would speak with him. When he was inclined to show me little acts of kindness, I accepted them in order to win him. Time after time I met him, and the opportunity to speak about the great question did not come.

When I was in Manchester, I referred to him and about my waiting for an opportunity, and a man in the audience said to another, "Well, he will die before he speaks to him."

But he was mistaken. I was watching and praying; God was listening, and the opportunity came. I returned from a mission and heard that this man had caught a cold and was quite ill. I met his daughter and asked if I could see her father. She said, "Yes; he heard that you were coming home and wondered if you would not come to see him."

I went to the room where he was lying in bed and found him very ill and very approachable. In fact, his wife was trying to read the Bible to him. I took the Bible and read passages that point out our need of a Savior, of God's love to us though we are sinners, and of God's way of salvation. I then explained the way of salvation and prayed with him. The next evening I met his daughter again and asked her if I could see her father again.

"Yes. He was hoping that you would come again and wondered if you would not." I heard that he had been talking about me and about my son, whose acquaintance he had also made. For part of the time he had been in delirium, and in his delirium he had been talking about my son. I went to see him and found him perfectly clear in mind, but I felt that he would not pull through the night. I was more specific than the night before and explained the way of life simply and fully, and he professed to accept Christ. I then knelt by his bed and prayed, and afterwards I asked him to follow me in prayer. Word by word, he followed me in the confession of his sin and in the expression of his belief in God's testimony about Jesus Christ – that Jesus had carried his sin in His own body on the tree. He asked God to forgive his sins, because Jesus had carried them in His own body on the cross. He told his heavenly Father that he trusted that He had forgiven his sins because of the atoning death of Christ. He told his Father that if it was His will, he wished to be raised from this bed of sickness in order to serve Christ, but that if it was not His will to raise him up, he was willing to be taken from this world – to depart and be with Christ. When I arose he seemed to be resting in the Lord Jesus. Two hours later there was a rap on my door, and a lady came in and told me that he had passed away trusting in Christ about an hour after I left.

> Eternity alone will reveal how many thousands have been won to Christ by the medium of letters from earnest Christians.

By letters

We cannot reach many people by a conversation, but we can reach them by letters. A letter is sometimes more effective than direct personal conversation. A letter can be read at leisure and apart by oneself, and it can be read again and again. Eternity alone will reveal how many thousands have been won to Christ by the medium of letters from earnest Christians. There is tremendous power in the pen. Have you consecrated your pen to Christ? You may not be able to write books, but you can write letters, and letters are often more effective than books. I know a woman in humble circumstances who makes a practice of writing letters to criminals in prison all over the United States. She has to do extra work to make the money to pay the postage for these letters, but her efforts have been greatly blessed by God. I have personally known a number of criminals in different states who have been won to Christ by the letters of this godly woman.

In one of our missions, one of the most prominent men in the town was just leaving the town as we arrived. In the good providence of God, the ship upon which he was sailing ran aground, and he had to return to the town. The next day was Sunday, and this man attended the meeting and was somewhat impressed. A leading lady of the town heard that he had been unable to get away and had been at the meeting, so she wrote him a letter urging him to accept Christ. This letter was accompanied by much prayer, and it did its work. This man came forward publicly and told the great throng of people that he had accepted Christ. His conversion made a great impression upon the whole community.

By tracts and booklets and books

There is great power in well-chosen tracts and books. The writer of one tract had letters from sixteen hundred people saying they had been brought to Christ by that tract. Sometimes you can hand a tract directly to those you wish to reach, but often you can reach people more effectively by indirection. They would be offended if you handed them a tract, but if you leave it around, they will pick it up out of curiosity and read it.

If there is an especially difficult case with someone, it is advantageous to invite him to your home. On the first night of his arrival, retire early but leave some well-chosen book that you wish him to read. Remove every other book from his room and provide a good light to read by. When he has been shown to his room at this unusually early hour, he will not wish to retire for the night. He will say, "Why do these people go to bed so early? I wonder if there is not something to read." He will look around and find there is only one book in the room. He will say, "It is a religious book," and will very likely add, "I don't care for religious books, but there is nothing else to read." He will sit down and begin to read that book. All this time you are in another room praying for him.

Sometimes it is best to put a tract under a person's pillow. When they are restless in the night, they feel the touch of that tract as they put their hand under their pillow. All men are naturally curious; they will turn on a light and read the tract and may be saved by it.

A young man in London was urged repeatedly by his godly mother to accept Christ. He was determined that he would not, and at last, to escape the unceasing pleadings of his mother, he left home and went to a town in the north of England. He obtained lodgings in this town. The woman with whom he obtained them was a godly woman. Seeing this young man away from home, her heart went out to him, and she put a tract under his pillow. When he went to bed that first night away from home, he was restless; putting his hand under his pillow, he felt the tract and wondered what it was. He turned on a light and found it was a religious tract. He said to himself, "Here I have run away from home to get rid of my mother's constant pleadings with me to become a Christian, and the first night away, I find a tract under my pillow; I might as well give in," and he did; he accepted Christ.

A friend of mine was once living in a godless home. When he left the home, he left his Bible behind with a tract in the Bible. After he had gone, out of curiosity, the lady of the house opened his Bible; it opened to where the tract lay, and she read it. She was converted by that tract. When he came back several days later for his Bible, he found that several members of the household had been led to Christ by the tract.

By such methods as these, and by all methods, by every kind of sanctified ingenuity, lay siege for those whom you have selected to win for Christ.

General Suggestions

A few general suggestions as to the spirit in which the work is to be done:

Be persistent

It is at this point that many would-be soul winners fail. They make one or two attempts to lead others to Christ, and these attempts appear to be unsuccessful, so they give up. No one can win souls to Christ in this way. The way to succeed in any kind of business is by persistence. A person can do most anything in this world that he makes up his mind to do if he will only stick to it. Stick-to-itiveness is a priceless grace, especially in soul winning. If one effort does not succeed, make another; if the second does not succeed, make another; if the hundredth effort does not succeed, make the hundred-and-first attempt. Don't give up until you win, if it takes fifty years.

I prayed and worked for the salvation of one man for fifteen years. I seemed to make absolutely no headway. He wandered further and further from God, but I did not give up. There could hardly be a more unlikely case than he was, utterly sunken in worldliness and sin, but I won. I had the joy of seeing that man become a preacher of the gospel, and today he is in heaven. When he was converted, his old friends could hardly believe it; it seemed preposterous to them that such a person had been converted, but he had. You can win anyone to Christ if you are willing to keep at it.

Be courteous

Nothing costs less, and few things pay better in this world than courtesy. It pays in business, but there is no place where it pays better than in soul-winning work. You may be poor, but you can be well bred. Treat every man with whom you deal as a gentleman and every woman with whom you deal as a lady.

I have seen people go at others in a most overbearing, discourteous, and irritating way. They assume an air of superiority. They treat the one with whom they are dealing as if he had no sense; they act as if they were determined to pound their ideas into another man's head. Now, every person of sense and character resents this kind of treatment. The person with whom you deal may be wrong, but you can treat his opinions and his feelings with consideration and kindness. You are far more likely to win him in that way. Never have heated arguments with those you wish to lead to Christ. Listen to what they have to say. Treat them with civility. It is quite possible to expose the hatefulness of another's sin in a courteous and considerate way. You will produce far deeper conviction in that way.

Never have heated arguments with those you wish to lead to Christ.

Avoid all intimacies with those with whom you are dealing. A gentleman or a lady always resents undue familiarity. I have seen a man sit down in our discussions after the meetings beside a young woman and put his arm along the back of the seat of the woman. Any lady resents such conduct and is likely to get up and leave the meeting. It is all right for a man to put his arm around a drunkard who has not had a kind action shown to him in years, as you kneel in prayer. It is all right for a lady to put her arm around a fallen sister who has had nothing but curses and abuse for years. It may be the first touch of a loving hand that she has had for many years and may soften her heart. But every worker must be careful to treat everyone with whom they deal with all due respect and courtesy.

Be earnest

Many would-be soul winners are utterly professional. Those with whom they deal cannot help but see that they have no real interest in their spiritual welfare and no deep concern for their souls. Such a worker may have a large technical knowledge of the Bible and of the right passages to use in dealing with certain classes of people, but his knowledge counts for nothing unless there is deep reality and earnestness behind it. Other workers may have a comparatively small knowledge of the Word but such an earnest love for the perishing that their little knowledge is used vastly beyond the superior knowledge of the other.

In a certain town lived an unbelieving blacksmith who was well read in secular literature and rejoiced in his power to defeat any opponent in argument. A deacon in the town had a great longing for this man's salvation. He studied the secular literature and the arguments to counter it. When he thought he had mastered the subject, he called upon this blacksmith to persuade him that he was wrong in his opinions, but he proved no match for the blacksmith. In a few moments, the blacksmith had shattered his arguments and defeated him utterly.

The deacon knew that he was right, but he could not prove it to the blacksmith. In his deep yearning for the salvation of the blacksmith, he burst into tears and said, "All I can say is that I have a great spiritual concern for your soul."

Then he left, went to his home, burst in upon his wife, and said, "Wife, I am a blunderer in God's work; God knows I really love that blacksmith's soul, and I went down to prove to him that he was wrong, but in a few minutes he beat me utterly in argument. I am only a blunderer in God's work."

He then retired to his room and knelt down to pray. He said, "O God, I am a failure in Your work. You know that I have a real desire for that man's salvation, but I have failed utterly in my attempt. I am a blunderer in Your work."

But soon after he had left the blacksmith's shop, the blacksmith went into his house and said to his wife, who was a godly woman, "Wife, Deacon was just over talking to me. He used one argument I did not understand. He said he had a great spiritual concern for my soul. What did he mean?"

His wife, who was a wise woman, said, "You had better go and ask him."

The blacksmith hung up his apron and went across the fields to the deacon's house. Just as he ascended the porch and was at the door, he heard the deacon in prayer saying that he was a failure in God's work. He pushed open the door and cried, "Deacon, you are no failure in God's work. I thought I knew all the arguments for Christianity and that I could answer them all, but you used an argument this morning I never heard before, and I cannot answer. You said you had a great spiritual concern for my soul."

The deacon had the joy immediately of leading that man to Christ. Have you a great spiritual concern for the souls of the perishing? If not, the sooner you get it, the better for you and for the lost.

Be winsome

A winsome manner goes a long way in soul winning. It is just as easy to smile as it is to scowl. It is just as easy to be cheerful and delightful as it is to be rude and repellent. Some people seem to take pride in their brusque, overbearing manner, but brusqueness is not a fruit of the Spirit. *The fruit of the Spirit is love, joy, peace, longsuffering, gentleness* (Galatians 5:22). A cheerful manner, the outcome of a life controlled by the Holy Spirit, is of more importance in soul winning than a theological education. Acts of kindness go a long way toward paving the way to the gate of a man's heart.

During visitation, a young missionary in Chicago found an unbeliever dying from tuberculosis. Day after day, she visited him with little gifts to make his last days on earth more pleasant. One day she'd bring a glass of jelly, another day something else. After about thirty days of such kind treatment, she became fearful that his time was short. She came to me at the close of my Bible class one Sunday afternoon and said, "Won't you come with me to see a dying man? I am afraid he will not live through the night."

I hurried with her to the poor room where the infidel lay dying. His wife was a Roman Catholic. I sat down by his bed and read the Scriptures to him, the Scriptures that make plain the love of God for sinners, the death of Christ in our place, and the way of salvation through our crucified Savior. I then asked him if I might pray with him, and he consented. I prayed God to open his eyes to show him that he was a lost sinner, but that Jesus had borne all his sins in His own body on the cross. Then I began to sing in a low tone by his bed –

> Just as I am, without one plea,
> But that Thy blood was shed for me,
> And that Thou bid'st me come to Thee,

O Lamb of God, I come! I come![6]

I sang it through, verse after verse, until I reached the last verse, and then I heard the dying infidel in a feeble voice join me in the verse –

> Just as I am, Thou wilt receive,
>   Wilt welcome, pardon, cleanse, relieve;
> Because Thy promise I believe,
>   O Lamb of God, I come, I come!

I looked up and asked him if he really had come. He said that he had. He passed into eternity that night. I was asked to conduct the funeral service. Standing by his casket with his unbelieving friends standing on the other side, I told how utterly insufficient his infidel views had proven in the time of crisis and of death, and how in those last hours he had accepted Christ. Then I said, "Who of you today will take the same step?"

> I doubt that there is a heart on earth that cannot be conquered by love.

One stalwart infidel reached his hand across the casket and said, "I will. I have sympathized with this man in his infidel views, but I give it up now and take Christ."

His wife also accepted Christ and today is a devoted member of our church in Chicago. But my brief visit did not win him to Christ. It was the kind, Christlike conduct of the young woman missionary.

Be full of love
Love is the first fruit of the Spirit, and it is the all-conquering power in soul-winning work. I doubt that there is a heart on earth that cannot be conquered by love. We have in America a

---

6   Charlotte Elliot, "Just As I Am," 1835.

devoted Christian woman of culture, refinement, and position who has a heart full of love for the most outcast and abandoned. She has devoted much of her life and strength to getting women appointed in jails and lockups for the reception and charge of female prisoners. Often she has found it hard work to convince the authorities to put a woman in charge of the female prisoners. In one city they said to her, "Mrs. Barney, no woman can manage the class of women with whom we have to do."

Mrs. Barney replied, "You never had a prisoner that I could not manage."

"We would like to have you try your hand on Old Sal," was the laughing reply.

"I would like to," replied the gentle lady.

"Well, the next time we have her under arrest, we will send for you."

Not long after, early one morning, Mrs. Barney received word that Old Sal was under arrest, so she hurried down to the lockup. She asked to be shown to Old Sal's cell.

The sergeant at the desk protested that it was not safe. "Look there," he said to Mrs. Barney, pointing to four policemen with torn clothes and faces. "There is a specimen of Old Sal's handiwork. It took these four men to arrest her."

"Never mind that," said Mrs. Barney. "Show me to her cell."

"Well, if you must go, an officer must go with you."

"No, I will go alone. Just let the jailer open the door, and I will go to her cell alone." Before going down Mrs. Barney had asked the sergeant at the desk for Old Sal's right name.

"Why," he said, "we always call her Old Sal."

"Yes," said Mrs. Barney, "but I wish to use her right name. What is her right name?"

"It is a long time since we first booked her, and we always book her now as Old Sal."

"Look up her right name," said Mrs. Barney.

The sergeant went back through the books and found Old Sal's proper name. The jailer opened the door and pointed to her cell down the corridor. When Mrs. Barney reached the door, she saw a wild creature with gray, torn hair, disheveled garments, and glaring eyes, crouching in the corner of the cell, waiting to spring upon the first policeman that should enter.

"Good morning, Mrs. (So-and-so)," said Mrs. Barney, calling her by her true name.

"Where did you get that name?" said the poor creature.

Without answering her question, Mrs. Barney said, "Sally, do you remember the first time you were committed here?"

"My God," she cried, "don't I! I spent the whole night crying on the floor of my cell."

"Suppose," said Mrs. Barney, "there had been some kind Christian woman here to have received you that night and to have treated you gently; do you think your life would have been different?"

"Altogether different," she replied.

"Well," said Mrs. Barney, "I am trying to get them to appoint a woman in this lockup to receive young girls when they are brought here for the first time, as you were when you were brought here that first night. Will you help me?"

"I will do all that I can," she said.

All the time Mrs. Barney had been drawing nearer and was now kneeling by her side on the cell floor, gathering up her torn and grizzled hair, fastening it up with pins taken out of her own hair, pulling together the torn shreds of her garments, and fastening them with pins taken from her own garments. The work was now done, and Mrs. Barney, rising to her feet, said, "Sally, we are going into the courtroom. If you will be good, they will appoint a woman in this lockup. Shall I go in on your arm, or will you go in on mine?"

The strong woman looked at Mrs. Barney and said, "I think

I am stronger than you are. You had better go in on my arm." And in they went to the court, the gentle lady leaning on the arm of the hardened old criminal. Sally restrained herself through the whole trial and answered the judge's questions pleasantly. She forgot herself once and swore at the judge, but immediately begged his pardon. Everybody was amazed at the transformation. A woman was appointed as matron of the jail, but best of all, Sally got her feet upon the Rock of Ages, and today Old Sal is in glory. Love had conquered. It always will.

Oh, men and women, young and old, go out to do this work. Seek the filling of the Spirit that God is so ready to give to us all, and in the power of that Spirit day after day, month after month, and year after year, labor on for the definite salvation of the specific souls that God shall bring your way. The time is getting short; let us make the most of it.

Reuben A. Torrey –
A Brief Biography

R euben A. Torrey was an author, conference speaker, pastor, evangelist, Bible college dean, and more. Reuben Archer Torrey was born in Hoboken, New Jersey, on January 28, 1856. He graduated from Yale University in 1875 and from Yale Divinity School in 1878, when he became the pastor of a Congregational church in Garrettsville, Ohio. Torrey married Clara Smith in 1879, with whom he had five children.

In 1882, he went to Germany, where he studied at the universities at Leipzig and Erlangen. Upon returning to the United States, R. A. Torrey pastored in Minneapolis, and was also in charge of the Congregational City Mission Society. In 1889, D. L. Moody called upon Torrey to lead his Chicago Evangelization Society, which later became the Moody Bible Institute. Beginning in 1894, Torrey was also the pastor of the Chicago Avenue Church, which was later called the Moody

Memorial Church. He was a chaplain with the YMCA during the Spanish-American War, and was also a chaplain during World War I.

Torrey traveled all over the world leading evangelistic tours, preaching to the unsaved. It is believed that more than one hundred thousand were saved under his preaching. In 1908, he helped start the Montrose Bible Conference in Pennsylvania, which continues today. He became dean of the Bible Institute of Los Angeles (now Biola University) in 1912, and was the pastor of the Church of the Open Door in Los Angeles from 1915 to 1924.

Torrey continued speaking all over the world and holding Bible conferences. He died in Asheville, North Carolina, on October 26, 1928.

R. A. Torrey was a very active evangelist and soul winner, speaking to people everywhere he went, in public and in private, about their souls, seeking to lead the lost to Jesus. He authored more than forty books, including *How to Bring Men to Christ, How to Pray, How to Study the Bible for Greatest Profit, How to Obtain Fullness of Power in Christian Life and Service*, and *Why God Used D. L. Moody*, and also helped edit the twelve-volume book about the fundamentals of the faith, titled *The Fundamentals*. He was also known as a man of prayer, and his teaching, preaching, writing, and his entire life proved that he walked closely with God.